Praise for Present th[...]

"Kirsten DeLeo has distilled timeless wisdom into a clear, accessible, and thoroughly helpful book. Rather than explain what to say or do, DeLeo shows us how to be with people who are approaching life's end. Her guidance is simple, practical, and profound: Show up. Arrive with love—for yourself and the person you are visiting. Lean forward. Listen. Remember to breathe."

　　—Ira Byock, MD, author of *Dying Well* and
　　　The Best Care Possible

"Kirsten DeLeo's *Present through the End* teaches essential lessons in the art of presence. This book is extraordinarily profound and yet simple as it leads the reader through practices to enhance listening, compassion, and mindfulness, and offers wise advice for negotiating the challenges of the dying process. With this inspirational book as a guide, care providers will transform death and dying for their patients and loved ones, while also deepening their own ability to create a sacred and healing space within."

　　—Karen Wyatt, MD, author of *What Really Matters*

"Through storytelling and rich personal experience, Kirsten DeLeo invites us to a more compassionate attitude toward death and our own mind. She teaches us how to walk gracefully with those who are dying and helps us befriend our fears of not being able to do enough. She shares the method, beauty, and power of simply being."

　　—Angela C. Anderson, MD, Brown University,
　　　Hasbro Children's Hospital

"Most of us come upon death unexpectedly and unprepared. So what to do? Kirsten DeLeo's book provides practical answers—compassionate, knowledgeable, heartfelt, doable. This is a book everyone needs to read; this is a book that can transform the experience of death."

—Ian Gawler, author of *Blue Sky Mind*

"Kirsten DeLeo's *Present through the End* is a must read for anyone who is caring for seriously ill patients or loved ones. Serious illness and the prospect of dying can trigger deep spiritual and existential suffering. Crying out in the presence of a sensitive listener can help the person eventually find peace but, even more importantly, experience love and acceptance. DeLeo offers readers simple, practical skills in being present to another and to ourselves. All clinicians, medical, nursing, and other health students need this guide to learn to integrate the art of presence in their clinical care."

—Christina M. Puchalski, MD, OCDS, George Washington University's Institute for Spirituality and Health, author of *Making Health Care Whole*

PRESENT
through the End

A Caring Companion's Guide *for* Accompanying *the* Dying

Kirsten DeLeo

SHAMBHALA BOULDER 2019

Shambhala Publications, Inc.
4720 Walnut Street
Boulder, Colorado 80301
www.shambhala.com

9 8 7 6 5 4 3 2 1

First Edition
Printed in the United States of America

♾ This edition is printed on acid-free paper that meets the
American National Standards Institute Z39.48 Standard.

♻ This book is printed on 30% postconsumer recycled paper.
For more information please visit www.shambhala.com.
Shambhala Publications is distributed worldwide by
Penguin Random House, Inc., and its subsidiaries.

Designed by Greta D. Sibley

Library of Congress Cataloging-in-Publication Data
Names: DeLeo, Kirsten, author.
Title: Present through the end: a caring companion's
guide for accompanying the dying/Kirsten DeLeo.
Description: First Edition. | Boulder, CO: Shambhala, 2019.
Identifiers: LCCN 2018059779 | ISBN 9781611807684 (paperback)
Subjects: LCSH: Older people—Care. | Older people—Family
relationships. | Death—Psychological aspects. | Bereavement. | BISAC:
FAMILY & RELATIONSHIPS / Death, Grief, Bereavement. | SELF-HELP
/ Death, Grief, Bereavement. | FAMILY & RELATIONSHIPS / Eldercare.
Classification: LCC HV1451.D445 2019 | DDC 649.8—dc23
LC record available at https://lccn.loc.gov/2018059779

To those who walk alongside the dying,

and who dare to be present with them.

CONTENTS

PRACTICES

Present through the End

INTRODUCTION

The first dying person I sat with was a young man, a twenty-eight-year-old cancer patient. He was the same age I was at the time. He had been in the hospital for many weeks for treatments to gain more time. His girlfriend had asked me to visit him when she learned that I was training as a hospice volunteer. Entering his barren, whitewashed hospital room, I felt utterly helpless and alone. The only thing I could do was to sit at his side and be present.

Death touches us all. At some point in our lives, most of us will find ourselves in the presence of someone who is facing death—a family member, friend, neighbor, or patient. Accompanying the dying, whatever our role, challenges us to be authentically and compassionately present and, ultimately, to look into the mirror of death ourselves and face the uncomfortable truth of our own mortality.

When we are with someone who is dying, we are challenged to be present even though we may feel powerless, to stay when we want to run, to love while loss is just around the corner, and to be fully alive to every moment as time is running out. Daring to be present might be the hardest thing we have ever done in our lives, and, we may come to discover, one of the most intimate, beautiful, and rewarding.

ABOUT THIS BOOK

Over the past twenty-five years, I have accompanied many people in different capacities as they faced the end of their lives. I have sat with family members, friends, hospice patients and clients, and complete strangers through the long hours of the night; I have attended them at home, in nursing homes, in the ICU, or in hospice. Someone who is dying needs a companion at their side who genuinely cares, who understands, and who is present without judgment. Those who walk alongside dying people also need a companion to be there for them along the way. I hope this book will help serve as that companion, offering support as you walk alongside someone at the end of life, no matter how difficult the process may feel.

Whether you are caring for a dying loved one, offering care in a professional role, or are preparing to support someone in the future, this book is for you. I hope this book will become your own kind and caring comforter and understanding friend, that it will be a go-to resource to help you navigate the difficult times ahead and inspire you to be present with an open heart.

In this book, you will find advice for every step of the way, from the moment when you first hear the news that someone is dying, right through to the time of their death, and beyond. The book is written in the style of "heart advice"—practical, pithy, down-to-earth guidance for real-life situations. The advice draws inspiration from many sources. It is based on my experience accompanying dying people, including work at the Zen Hospice, Laguna Honda Hospital and Maitri in San Francisco, and the Spiritual Care Centers in Ireland and in Germany. It draws inspiration from the practical and profound wisdom of my Buddhist teachers and many years of immersion in Buddhist contemplative practice. The book is also inspired by my experience teaching caregivers around the world and the work of the Spiritual Care Programme and Authentic Presence, a course in contemplative end-of-life care I helped to pioneer and have been teaching with a great team since 2003. I hope the advice will be helpful to any of you seeking support as you accompany someone through the end of life—whether you are familiar with Buddhism, another religious tradition, or practice no spiritual tradition at all.

In my care for dying people, I have found Buddhist teachings—namely, Tibetan Buddhism and its approach to train the human heart and mind—incredibly valuable and effective. In Buddhism, death is viewed as a natural part of life, a reality we can learn to accept and even make friends with. The actual moment of death, instead of being reduced to a mere physical or medical event, is honored as sacred.

Contemplative thought and practices have radically transformed my ability to be present for another and befriend my own mind. On the most profound level, they have given me trust and confidence in the human capacity for boundless, fearless compassion and wisdom—a capacity that radiates from a deeper, spiritual source of who we are. It has taught me the most important lesson in accompanying dying people and in much of the rest of life: *it is not what you say or do that counts, but how you are.*

HOW TO USE THIS BOOK

I hope you can pick up this book whenever you need guidance, inspiration, and encouragement. Each chapter walks you through some aspect of being present for someone at the end of life—from what to say (or not) when you don't know what to say, to what to do when the moment of death arrives. Throughout each chapter you will find inspiration from spiritual teachers, contemplative thinkers, and poets—insights that have nourished my soul and uplifted my spirits in difficult times and, I hope, will do the same for you. You will also find moving statements from dying people on what matters most to them. The names of patients have been changed, also some of the details, to ensure their privacy.

Most chapters also include short, easy-to-do "on-the-spot" practices that can be done in a moment, whether at home, at the bedside, or wherever you need them. I hope these practices will help you find peace or presence when you need them most. These on-the-spot practices include short meditations and guided contemplations—practical tools inspired by Buddhist tradition and our long experience in the international Spiritual Care Programme. I have shared these exercises with thousands of professional and volunteer caregivers around the world. You do not need any background in Buddhism or meditation to benefit from them. The practices are most effective if you do them regularly, for short sessions of five to ten minutes. They will help you to stay sane, grounded, and calm in the midst of uncertainty, to be open with all that arises in your experience, and at the same time to hold the space for the dying person.

Scientific studies are beginning to discover how these practices reduce stress and anxiety, help us process our emotions, and transform how we relate to others. A number of studies have specifically focused on caregivers or health-care professionals. They indicate very clearly that there are some simple things we can do to protect ourselves from stress and burnout, and connect better with those we care for.

Please approach the book as it calls to you. Read the book straight through, or choose a section that feels most relevant to your circumstances or addresses a specific question that you are facing. You can read the book anytime, anywhere: while getting ready to make the first call to a friend who has just been diagnosed with a life-threatening illness, while waiting in a doctor's office, or during your lunch break. You can glide over the poetic interludes and go straight to the practical information, or vice versa. You can turn to the lists of conversation starters or questions when you feel at a loss for how to address a difficult topic. You can return to a favorite practice when you need to steady yourself before approaching the bedside. Or you can go through the following pages at a more leisurely pace—over a cup of tea, with time to think more about the pieces that hold your interest and invite you to take a deep breath.

If you find anything helpful, please use it and share it with others. If something does not make sense or is not relevant to your situation, that's fine too. It might be useful for someone else.

Supporting a fellow human being to die well and to extend your kindness is both difficult and beautiful, ordinary and deeply spiritual. We don't need to be helpless and unprepared when facing death—others' or our own. There are skillful ways in which we can grow and deepen the wisdom of the heart to meet the actual moment not empty-handed.

This small guide is more than a book. It is a companion you can carry with you. Walking alongside dying people, we can often feel helpless and isolated. Know that you are not alone.

1

The Power of a Loving Presence

"I am scared. I want to be there but seeing him die is just too hard," said my friend in a low voice when I picked up the phone. Her father had been living with cancer for a long time, and now he was dying from it. My friend's honest statement encapsulates the deep helplessness we face when we are confronted with dying and the powerful wish to be there for the person, if only we knew how. Being present with dying people is not something we are taught growing up at home or in school, and even medical education lacks professional training that acknowledges the human aspect and inner, spiritual dimension of both life and death. Individually, and as a society, we are ill-equipped to be present for those in our midst who are at the threshold of life and death, to care for them and respond to their inner needs and deeper questions.

The image of walking alongside, or accompaniment, for me beautifully captures the essence of what we do when we care for someone who is nearing death. It honors the natural human quality of caring for another and recognizes that loss, illness, and death are shared human experiences, without disregarding the need for professional expertise and knowledge.

My experience with John, a close friend who died of AIDS, helped teach me this lesson about the importance of human care and connection at the end of life. John was one of San Francisco's longtime survivors. As his condition worsened and it became clear that he wouldn't make it through his latest health crisis, John decided to leave the hospital so he could die at home, supported by his community and a few close friends. When I came over to visit him the first afternoon he was home, I asked him what I could do to help. "Just be my friend," he said, with some sadness. The simplicity of his statement touched me and everyone else who was present with him that afternoon. His words brought home what caring is all about.

Being a companion to someone who is dying ultimately has nothing to do with responsibilities or roles. Just like being a good friend, it simply means we are willing to listen and be present to the unique experiences of a fellow human being, and how that person chooses to fill these experiences with meaning.

And yet, though it might sound simple, being present with dying people can be difficult for so many reasons. I was fortunate to learn from my grandmother how to be around a dying person. My grandfather was ninety-two years old when he died, and my grandmother and I took care of him in his final days. He died on a Sunday morning, at home, in his own bed, surrounded by his family. We sat by his side, and when the time came, we washed his body and dressed him in his best Sunday suit. All of this was done with great love and tenderness. My grandmother asked for his body to remain at home for one more night. She slept next to his body, as she had done for the past seventy years, and I curled up next to them, like I used to when I was a child.

For my grandmother, death was a natural thing. There was deep sadness, of course, but it did not have the power to take away her love. In the way that she cared for my grandfather she taught me an ordinary, yet profound, lesson: the power of a loving presence.

YOU ARE ALL THAT IS NEEDED

When someone is seriously ill and facing death, we want to help, but we may not know how. We may worry that we don't know enough or feel afraid that we might make things worse. We ask ourselves: *What if I do or say something wrong?* These are very real and understandable fears, but this doesn't mean we should let them prevent us from being present.

Life is messy, and we do make mistakes. Even with our mistakes, being present with a kind heart and good intentions can be a blessing for dying people. Early one morning, I got a phone call from hospice. One of my patients just had suffered a severe panic attack. When I arrived she had already calmed down somewhat, but was still restless and talking incessantly, one thought on top of another. A heavy feeling of fear permeated the room. I felt centered—aware of my body and anchored in the natural calm flow of my breath. Yet, there was one part of me that felt great unease witnessing the depth of her anxiety and wanted so much to make things okay. Against my better judgment, I tried to talk her out of how she was feeling, downplaying her desperate situation and pushing away her concerns. To no one's surprise, what I said was less than helpful. It made her even more upset. When I finally recognized the unhealthy dynamic of our exchange, I paused and took a deep breath. There was no way to make her situation okay or safe. She was dying and she was afraid. "I am sorry," I said. "What I am saying sucks, doesn't it? I am sorry for how you feel. This must be scary." She nodded and leaned her head against my shoulder. I took her hand and held it gently and offered her the support of my body while I continued to listen, sending her loving-kindness (a practice we'll explore shortly) until she regained a calmer state of mind.

Perhaps it is difficult for us to consider and even trust that our presence alone could be all that is needed because there is this nagging voice in the background telling us that we are not good enough. Not believing that our presence is sufficient, we overcompensate by doing too much. We put pressure on ourselves to try to make things right again when they never can be, but also as a way to manage our deep sense of discomfort with suffering and pain. It's natural not to know what to do in these painful situations. Just being there is what matters most. Or, as Woody Allen said, 80 percent of success is showing up. We don't need to improve ourselves into something better like so many self-help books and lifestyle gurus want to make us believe, assuming our presence and who we are is fundamentally lacking something. You *are* good enough, and your kind and caring presence is all that you need.

When people experience deep suffering, what helps them most of all—more than anything we can say or do—is *how we are*. What matters most is love: being a loving, caring presence for the dying person. To be present and listen is often all that it takes. This does not mean it is easy. But the ability to be present with someone who is in emotional or spiritual pain is the most beautiful thing that we can give to one another as human beings. A quote attributed to Maya Angelou powerfully captures the benefit and grace of presence: "I've learned that people will forget what you said, people will forget what you did, but people will never forget how you made them feel."

> Often when a physician cannot imagine what else to do for someone who is feeling helpless and hopeless—for whom life has no value—I find that love is the answer.
>
> —Ira Byock, *The Best Care Possible*

Dame Cicely Saunders, one of the pioneers of the modern hospice movement, told a moving story that illustrates perfectly the need for us to care genuinely. "I once asked a man who knew he was dying what he needed above all in those who were caring for him. He said, 'For someone to look as if they are trying to understand me.' Indeed, it is impossible to understand fully another person, but I never forget that he did not ask for success but only that someone should care enough to try."

Your willingness and heart's courage to be there, to listen and care—even though you do not always have the answers and cannot fix the situation—in itself can have a tremendously calming and reassuring effect on the mind and heart of the dying person. All they need is someone who stays present no matter what, who is real and, most importantly, kind. You do not have to be perfect. You do not have to be an expert. All you need to do is care enough to try.

COURAGE TO CARE

Those who are dying, especially right after receiving their diagnosis, may feel groundless and too overwhelmed to put their experience into words. When we first visit, they may feel unsure about how to open up, and wonder about our intentions. We too can feel groundless. We can feel insecure and reserved, not knowing what to say or do, and how to be. Experiencing groundlessness is, in fact, a good thing. However uncomfortable or painful, it is an invitation to stay open, to drop any agenda or concept about what should happen. "The bad news is you're falling through the air, nothing to hang on to, no parachute," Chögyam Trungpa told his students. "The good news is, there's no ground."

I know this sounds counterintuitive, but when you feel groundless, the main thing to do is to relax. Just be yourself, be natural, and relax. Nothing extraordinary needs to happen. A heartfelt connection comes with good intention, in the ordinary moments of life, in simple, ordinary ways—and that is what is extraordinary. In chapter 2 we'll look at some practices for when you feel groundless that can help you connect with your good intentions and feel more at ease. The most meaningful interactions happen when we stop trying too hard, trying to be too wise, and touch our own vulnerability. When we do, we have the opportunity to discover something much deeper within ourselves, something that lies beyond all our worries, concerns, and fears.

Paradoxically, caring for another person is not about us providing that person with something. If we approach the act of caring as though we are giving something to someone who is weaker than ourselves, we will never relate to another as a whole person.

We cannot *do* loving, authentic presence. If we try, it feels fake and sentimental, like an empty gesture devoid of true meaning and heart. We can only *be* a loving, authentic presence. It is a way of being—an understanding of the deeper inner dimension of who we are as human beings, a recognition of the fundamental openness, clarity, and love that lies within each of us.

Whether we accompany someone in a professional role or as a family member or friend, it always takes a degree of courage. There is no doubt about that. It takes courage to be at the bedside with all our human flaws and imperfections, our fears and self-concerns, and sometimes our feelings of deep helplessness. But when someone cares for us deeply it gives us hope, and when we care deeply for someone it gives us strength and confidence. The Tibetan word for *courage*, translated literally, means "heart bone." The metaphor points to the confidence and the great physical strength of heart—the bone at the heart—that is needed both in order to be present with someone who is experiencing suffering and to face our own reactions as we bear witness.

Confidence is not something that we already need to have perfected before we start to care for a dying person. It is something *that grows by caring*, by simply showing up and staying close. Walking alongside transforms the experience of the dying person, and we are transformed as well. It gives us the opportunity to discover an inner capacity for kindness, compassion, and wisdom that we may never have suspected we possessed, even though is has always been ours. The next chapter looks at ways you can build your courage and tap into your good intentions to care.

2

Preparing to Care

"I don't think I can do this!"

Perhaps this was the first thought that went through your mind when you heard the sad news and you are about to visit for the first time. That's okay. Most of the time, by simply acknowledging these feelings, they lose their power over us.

It is important, as much as possible, to have an open and clear mind when we are in the presence of a person who is facing death. What we bring into the room—our thoughts and feelings—can have a tremendous impact, positive or negative. If you are anxious, this can become part of the other's experience. Likewise, if you are at ease, grounded, and open, this atmosphere of confidence will communicate itself. Daijaku Kinst, a friend and Zen Buddhist teacher, poignantly summed it up, "The first step in any care relationship is being less anxious than the person one is serving."

Knowing we should not bring our anxiety into the presence of dying people is one thing, but actually achieving this can be another. Fortunately, there are ways we can work with our thoughts and feelings that both acknowledge the realities of our challenging experience and also help us find enough inner stability to support someone else.

> For one human being to love another: that is perhaps the most difficult of all our tasks; the ultimate, the last test and proof, the work for which all other work is but preparation.
> —Rainer Maria Rilke, *Letters to a Young Poet*

BEING SPACIOUS WITH THOUGHTS AND EMOTIONS

Be kind and spacious with the thoughts and emotions that rise in your mind, and don't judge what comes up. If you have just received the painful news that someone close to you is facing death, for example, all sorts of disturbing thoughts and feelings can surface. This is completely natural, and part of the process of coming to terms with the new reality. Experiences of sadness, anger, fear, confusion, numbness, or grief can come in waves, and often when you least expect them. We can be sitting on the bus, in the middle of a conversation with a colleague, or walking down the street. We can take heart that these are universal experiences—the poem "The Guest House" by Rumi illustrates well how emotions can arise and pass, and how we can be present with them without judgment.

The Guest House

This being human is a guest house.
Every morning a new arrival.

A joy, a depression, a meanness,
some momentary awareness comes
as an unexpected visitor.

Welcome and entertain them all!
Even if they are a crowd of sorrows,
who violently sweep your house
empty of its furniture,
still, treat each guest honorably.
He may be clearing you out
for some new delight.

The dark thought, the shame, the malice.
meet them at the door laughing
and invite them in.

Be grateful for whatever comes,
because each has been sent
as a guide from beyond.

> —Rumi, *The Essential Rumi*,
> translation by Coleman Barks

It can really help to consider whatever myriad thoughts or emotions that arise simply as experiences that are passing through our awareness. The main point is not to fixate by identifying with them. These feelings are not who we are; they just come and go. Our capacity to simply be aware is linked to our natural awareness that is always present, but is often hidden behind the constant flow of things that pass through our busy mind. We can compare the nature of mind to the sky, the thoughts and emotions to the clouds that move through it. I love Pema Chödrön's no-nonsense reminder, "You are the sky. Everything else—it's just the weather." By connecting with our ever-present but often-hidden natural awareness, we connect with a greater sense of stability and calmness. We tap into our innermost essence or deeper space within our being—clear, compassionate, and open—from which we can hold a healing space for another. This takes practice, but it is possible.

> Quietly sitting, body still, speech silent, mind at ease and at peace, you simply let thoughts and emotions, whatever arises, come and go, without clinging to them.
>
> —*The Tibetan Book of Living and Dying*

> Without a center, without an edge . . . without an inside, without an outside . . . as far as the sky pervades, so does awareness.
>
> —Shabkar, *The Life of Shabkar: The Autobiography of a Tibetan Yogin*

You can try the following practice whenever you feel overcome by difficult thoughts or emotions. You can do it right in the moment you begin to feel overwhelmed, whether you are alone or in the presence of the dying person. This practice is about just being present with and noticing how things are for us—learning to observe thoughts, feelings, and perceptions as they are. We cannot force our minds into peacefulness, however hard we try. By simply being aware and noticing, by giving space and being self-aware instead of reacting, we can learn to manage difficult mental and emotional states. We can try being a neutral observer of what's happening in our minds. As an observer it may become easier to dissolve or drop difficult feelings or thoughts, or at least to lower their noise level so we can act with greater clarity, genuine care, and kindness.

Sometimes, it can be easier to settle into a calmer place within ourselves when we are alone. If you find yourself in a situation with other people around and you realize things are just too much and you need time alone, be kind to yourself. Don't hesitate to excuse yourself for a few moments. Do this short practice until you feel more settled and are ready to engage again.

FINDING A PLACE OF CALM

When you notice a wave of sadness, fear, negativity, or anxiety rising, pause for a moment, sit down, and just watch what is happening like a neutral observer. Feel yourself centered in your body—notice the feeling of your feet on the floor, the air on your skin—and stay with the natural flow of your breath. In and out. In and out. And again, in and out. Allow the experience to wash over you like a wave, and keep breathing deeply. Like waves, these feelings rise and they subside again. Try to neither follow your thoughts or emotions nor indulge them. Simply be aware. Observe and be mindful of your experience, without evaluating what is happening as good or bad.

If your thoughts and emotions are particularly strong,

imagine yourself like the ocean looking at its own waves. Your awareness is as vast as the ocean. There is the natural movement of the ocean's waves, and at the same time underneath the waves, there is a deep stillness. Or you can imagine yourself like the sky gazing down on the clouds that pass across it. Imagine being as expansive and open as the sky, and allow the cloud-like thoughts to come and go.

Choose the image that resonates with you the most and stay with it for a while. Notice the atmosphere it evokes in your mind, your body, and your heart, and remain mindful, open, and aware. Try to remain in this atmosphere for a few moments longer.

GETTING SUPPORT

As you prepare to care, make sure to get support and reach out to your local hospice- and palliative-care services. The goal of palliative and hospice care is to provide comfort for anyone with a serious illness. Both palliative and hospice care aim to prevent or treat symptoms and minimize the side effects of disease and treatment. They can also support you in dealing with emotional, social, practical, or spiritual concerns that illnesses can bring up, for the dying person as well as yourself.

A patient can receive palliative care as soon as the illness is diagnosed, when receiving treatments meant to cure or treat the disease, during follow-up, and at the end of life. This care is available to hospital patients whether or not they have decided to stop treatments aimed at life extension. Hospice care, on the other hand, is for people who are no longer receiving treatment to cure their illness and may only have weeks or months to live. It can be administered at home or in a hospital.

It may be helpful to have an honest conversation with medical providers and to ask about a referral to palliative care. Many hospitals have palliative-care consultation teams that can help you to assess the options. If the person is dying at home, you can request an information visit from a hospice agency. The "Resources" section at the end of the book can help you find additional information on palliative and hospice care to make decisions that support the dying person's end-of-life wishes. When your loved one feels supported and knows you are too, it will improve their quality of life. Likewise, it will give you much-needed peace of mind.

CONNECTING WITH YOUR GOOD HEART

Before you visit the dying person, always inspire yourself first by connecting with your compassionate motivation, your good heart. This only takes a few seconds, but it makes a world of difference. Our intentions are reflected in the way we care, in our verbal and our nonverbal communication, in the way we touch or gaze at the person. That is why it is so important to clarify our intention and establish our motivation as we start each day, and with each interaction.

Before entering the room, take a moment to check if you are going in with any hidden hopes and fears—expectations, agendas, or worries. Inevitably, without mindful awareness these hopes and fears—however subtle—can be a barrier to making a genuine connection with the dying person. By examining our intentions, we might, for example, realize that we are going to someone's bedside out of a sense of duty or obligation, rather than our genuine wish. Or, we might find that we want to push our agenda. We should treat whatever we find not as a stick to beat ourselves with but as a valuable discovery. When you find that your frame of mind is not as open or positive as it could be, instead of becoming self-critical, simply use it as a chance to adjust your mental attitude to one that is more beneficial. Quietly holding an intention that we will do our best can do the trick. Even if we don't quite feel we are in a good place yet, as long as we hold this kind of clear intention in mind and keep working on cultivating a compassionate motivation, it is fine to proceed.

Everything depends on your intention.

All the time, therefore, check your attitude and motivation.

> —Dilgo Khyentse Rinpoche,
> *The Heart of Compassion*

Real care of the sick does not begin with costly procedures, but with the simple gift of affection and love. In the practice of healing, a kind heart is as valuable as medical training, because it is the source of happiness for both oneself and others. People respond to kindness even when medicine is ineffective, and in turn cultivating a kind heart is a cause of our own good health.

> —The Dalai Lama, foreword to *Healing Images*

When we connect with compassionate motivation, we connect with our greatest inner resource: our basic goodness. The more we can come in touch with our basic goodness and rest in it, the more courage and natural confidence we will have to relate to the dying person with honesty and without fear. Our presence and love then has the power to offer genuine comfort and reassurance. When we allow these qualities to shine through, it creates a safe environment in which the dying person can relax and rest. Our strength and calmness, our warmhearted attention, can awaken that person's own inner strength. The following practice can help you check in with your intention.

SETTING YOUR INTENTION

Before you visit, pause for a moment and become mindful of your intentions. Are there any hidden hopes and fears? Are there any expectations, agendas, or worries that could get in the way? Simply recognize them, and let them go, without judging yourself. Then take a moment to connect with your compassionate motivation, your good heart, and consciously establish your motivation for what you are about to do. You can use a phrase like this: *May what I do or say be of benefit and help to relieve suffering.*

Whenever you feel you are getting worried about what you can do or say, shift your thinking from the question of "What can *I* do?" to "What do *you* need?" This internal shift in perspective from "I" to "you," from your needs to the other's needs, will bring you right back to your compassionate motivation.

GETTING IN TOUCH WITH
YOUR CAPACITY TO CARE

Perhaps the idea of feeling connected to your good heart, your capacity to care, and your basic goodness sounds too abstract, unattainable, or even sentimental. Whatever we choose to call it, this compassionate motivation certainly does not always come easily, and the connection seems to flicker on and off. We can have a hard time recognizing and appreciating our own ability and capacity for love and compassion. At the start, even if it feels strange or contrived to intentionally connect with your compassionate motivation—your good heart—still, give it a try. It is only a thought, that's true, but this thought has the power to change our attitude; and, by changing our attitude, the way we perceive a situation and other people will change as well.

Compassion means letting go of your self-identity, letting go of proving that identity all the time. Compassion means you work in the way the wind works, the sun works, or the air works. Take, for example, how the air assumes the shape of the room. The air does not say, "I will give you this breathing space provided you breathe the way I want." Everyone enjoys the benefit of being able to breathe in the air. It is the same way with the sun: the sun does not stop shining when there are clouds in the sky.

In that same way, selflessness free from attachment, or compassion used with wisdom, means that one goes beyond the way *you* want to do things. If you can let go of making yourself the most important person in the world, there will be more capacity and spaciousness within you to work with others. You will find more space, time and energy within yourself.

—Khandro Rinpoche, *Lion's Roar*

It might not always feel like we care, but our willingness to be present with dying people, no matter what, shows that we do. In times when I feel hard-hearted, closed off, resentful, cynical, self-critical, or discouraged, the following exercise has always helped me to soften these attitudes and reach back into a feeling of caring.

RECALLING YOUR GOODNESS

Bring to mind a situation when you felt you were able to be present for another person, a moment when your heart went out to a fellow human being who was struggling and having a hard time. This memory does not have to be anything heroic or grand. It can be a small gesture of human kindness or attention, an understanding and feeling of warmth that you showed to someone who needed it. Bring this situation vividly to mind, and remember how you felt at the time. Allow these feelings of warmth, generosity, and connection to soften and dissolve any hard-heartedness, and stay with that memory for a while longer. Let these feelings in. No matter who we are, we all have the capacity to love and care for each other.

SEEING OTHERS AS JUST ANOTHER YOU

I worked for many years at Laguna Honda, one of the last nursing facilities in San Francisco with open wards. In the hospice ward, I experienced for the first time viscerally how we are all the same when facing aging, illness, and dying. The hospice ward was one large room with twenty-eight beds: men at one end, women at the other, each separated from the others by only a flimsy curtain. The patients came from very diverse cultural and spiritual backgrounds. The suffering of the entire world seemed to be enclosed by the four walls of this ward. It made my heart ache. Despite the sadness, there was an underlying feeling that we are all connected, that no one was alone in their suffering. Patients who were still well enough to get around sat at the bedsides of those who were leaving ahead of them. Any separation between me and the other had evaporated. The other was simply another you experiencing the inevitable future we all share. Here, in this place, among the fellowship of the dying, I learned what it meant to "bear witness" and about the profound beauty of our human brokenness.

The poet Rainer Maria Rilke described our deepest fears as dragons guarding our deepest treasure. Being with the dying continuously challenges us to get to know ourselves, our heart and mind, and to bear witness—to be open, aware, and present.

When you think about coming face-to-face with change and death, you are inevitably working with your own states of mind, just as the dying person is. Perhaps you feel vulnerable, tearful, helpless, paralyzed, or simply uneasy. The dying person may feel the very same way.

"I think it is tempting to distance yourself from a patient and make of them a group of symptoms and diagnoses," acknowledged one of the physicians in a workshop I taught at a hospital. "However, that's not what we're called upon to do, since the patient is looking for healing, not just treatment."

I fear that you will forget who I am.

Even though I am facing death, I am still living. I want people to treat me normally and to include me in their lives.

I want you to see me as a whole person, not as a disease, or a tragedy, or a fragile piece of glass. Do not look at me with pity but rather with all of your love and compassion.
—Voices of dying people

In the months before my mother died, she was undergoing chemo treatment at a large teaching hospital. One morning when I was visiting, she was silently crying. When

I asked what was the matter, she said, "They don't see me. They don't see me." Nurses and doctors had come in and out all morning, mostly avoiding eye contact getting through their tasks. They examined her, lifted her body skillfully, purposefully, and efficiently. Even with all their medical expertise, however, their behaviors also expressed discomfort at being around a very ill person. They moved my mother's body without really touching her. They looked at my mother without truly seeing her. My mother wasn't any longer a person, but had become a patient. Not only that—a patient who was terminal.

People with a terminal illness can experience profound isolation and loneliness. Like my mother, they feel they have become invisible to the world. One young man I accompanied mentioned that, with his diagnosis, with the labels "incurable" and "terminal," it was as though he had crossed a hidden threshold from the realm of the living to the dying. Suddenly most everyone he knew—relatives, friends, acquaintances, neighbors, and coworkers, including health-care professionals—started to behave and speak differently. "They tiptoe around me now, speaking over me rather than with me in hushed voices and serious demeanor," he said. "But I am still here."

When we prepare to care, we should remember that a dying person is still a person, a fellow human being—not a "special category" or a "project." Their situation might have changed, but the person is still the same. If we can stop for a minute to see the person rather than the disease, if we can try to recognize the true nature of the person, beyond the signs and symptoms of illness or approaching death, this will have a profound impact. This will make them feel like a living and loved being right up until the end.

One of my mentors and supportive friends, Christine Longaker, who has been a pioneer in the field of caring for the dying for over forty years, has identified four essential inner or spiritual needs that we all share, and which become especially important for someone who is dying. In her thoughtful book *Facing Death and Finding Hope*, she calls them the "four tasks of living and dying":

- To understand and transform one's experience of suffering
- To experience authentic connection and love
- To feel one's life is meaningful
- To rely on a refuge or source of peace

Considering these basic needs of feeling loved and cared for, of knowing that we matter, and of being connected to those around us and even something bigger than ourselves to cope with suffering, we are not so different.

When you think about the person you are caring for,

whether it is a relative or someone you have just met, as "just another you"—just another human being with the same hopes and same fears—it will immediately soften your heart. It will give rise to feelings of closeness and warmth and melt away feelings of anxiety, insecurity, and separation. This is helpful to remember when you are preparing to care, and it's also true at the bedside. Seeing yourself in another person is not about projecting or assuming too much of your own situation in someone. We do need to be sensitive to realities of race, cultural or economic backgrounds, gender, sexual orientation, beliefs, generational differences, and so on, as we embrace our common humanity. This reflection is not whitewashing differences. Instead, connecting with another person as "another you" can help to raise awareness and increase empathy because it wears down the self-centered and self-absorbed attitudes that obstruct more inclusive and understanding perspectives. If you are a professional caregiver, I have found that considering the dying person as another you is a simple yet effective way to prevent care from becoming routine, and the person you care for from becoming just another case or number.

If you are feeling disconnected from the person you are caring for, you can consider the following practice before you arrive at the bedside. It is also very powerful when you are in the presence of another person.

JUST ANOTHER YOU

See the dying person not in their usual role as father or mother, patient or client, but as *just another you*—as someone who is not so different from you.

Consider these statements:

"Just like me, this person is trying to avoid suffering."

"Just like me, this person wants to be happy."

"Just like me, this person has fears."

"Just like me, this person has hopes, dreams, and wishes; good memories, strengths, and accomplishments; things to live for and enjoy."

STEPPING INTO THE OTHER PERSON'S SHOES

A step further than seeing someone as another you is to put yourself into that person's shoes. Considering this practice can be very helpful if you know you might struggle to understand a dying person's behavior, and you are concerned about how to be in that person's presence, how you will understand their needs, or how you will respond. You can start by simply trying to see the person as another you and then, as a further step, put yourself in their shoes. We never really understand other people until we consider things from their point of view—until we put ourselves in their shoes and walk around in them.

The following reflection can be very helpful any time you are feeling blocked in caring for someone, especially a family member or a friend with whom you might have a difficult history, or a person who is no longer able to communicate because of progressive illness, for example. Undoubtedly, we can never know anyone completely. But love has the power to connect us.

IN THE OTHER PERSON'S SHOES

Imagine yourself living this person's life, with their present experiences of suffering.

Imagine as well that you have this person's history. This includes accomplishments and good memories, but also difficult experiences and worries they may have about the future. These might include concerns about physical deterioration, increasing dependence, loss of control or economic worries, fears of physical pain and dying, and spiritual distress.

Try seeing the world through this person's eyes, and ask yourself:

What would I most want from the person who is coming to see me?

What would I most need from that person?

How would I want the person coming into the room to view me?

Practicing this reflection before you approach the person who needs care can help open you to the possibility of connection with someone with whom it seems difficult to connect, or someone you are no longer sure you understand. Together, I hope the ideas and practices in this chapter help you prepare yourself in the important work of walking alongside someone at the end of life.

3

Present at the Bedside

Charles, a man in his seventies, was one of my first hospice patients. I had been sitting with him during the afternoon, and I was coming to the end of my work shift. It was the end of a summer day, and I still remember how the red shadows from the setting sun enveloped his room and touched his dark skin. His eyes were closed, and he spoke softly in between long pauses to catch his breath. I listened. *I don't know this old man*, I thought. I had only seen him a few times. We were just two strangers, sitting together. Looking at this frail body, I felt sad and tender.

As I tried to let go of his hand gently and lean back on my chair into the shadows of the room to hide my face and feelings, he suddenly shifted his head toward me and opened his eyes. It felt like I had just walked into a fire. *Don't run. Just don't run. Stay*, an inner voice said. Without a word, he pulled my hand onto his chest and rested it there. I could feel the bones underneath his skin, his heartbeat. *This is what it means to be present*, I realized in that moment. *Not to run, but to stay, even in the fiercest fire.* I moved back out of the shadows so he could see my face. My heart burned, but at its very center was a place of unexpected calmness. "I am sad. I am here," I said to him. He gently squeezed my hand. "Good," he said. "Good." With his small gesture of resting my hand on his chest and his kind, simple reassurance—through his presence—Charles taught me how to be present for others. He showed me that it was okay to feel vulnerable, and still show up. He taught me how to stay when I wanted to run, to remain open when I felt sad or afraid.

Living and dying happen in the present moment. Being at someone's bedside is a continual reminder to stay in the moment, to slow down, and be.

The dying are losing their entire world, and may be sicker than they have ever been in their life. They may no longer be able to think clearly, to carry out daily tasks, and they may be unable to support themselves physically. Their outer world is continually becoming smaller and smaller, and they experience life in the slow lane. Confined to a bed, they are no longer in charge of their own lives in the way they used to be. What matters to them now are little things, the things that we often don't notice because we are speeding along in the fast lane, planning what comes next.

REMEMBER TO SLOW DOWN

When we slow down, we will be better attuned to the needs of the dying person, and we will also feel more connected to ourselves. Every so often, don't we feel that we keep missing each other—and ourselves—because our life is going too fast?

A kind gaze, a gentle touch, the afternoon sunlight streaming into the room, the noise of the garbage truck in the street, the laughter of the children playing outside—these are the kind of things that begin to matter more and more. As the dying person's physical world is becoming smaller, their inner world can deepen, grow, and become tremendously rich. This may sound surprising, but dying is an opportunity for growth—an opportunity for *growing inward.*

For a dying family member, friend, or patient, our inner restlessness or speediness will feel like impatience or, even worse, rejection and aggression. When we slow down, we shift from human *doing* to human *being.* This can be deeply relaxing and rewarding, not only for the dying person, but for us as well. There are so many precious and tender moments in our life that we would have missed had we been in a hurry.

So how can we slow down, right here, right now?

MINDFULNESS OF THE BODY

You can try this practice any time you need to pause, to slow down, to become present. You can try the practice for a few moments, or you can sit with it longer to deepen the experience.

Become mindful of your body. Bring your awareness to your head, and then your face.

Notice your breath, and the sensation of the natural flow of your breath.

Bring mindful awareness to your neck, and then to your shoulders, your arms, your chest, your belly.

Feel the weight of your body sitting in the chair, and then feel the sensation in your legs and feet.

Simply feel your body, inside and out.

Just notice, and pay attention without judgment.

This mindful attention will help you to slow down, and also help you to calm your nervous system, so that you can become more in tune with yourself and feel more present for the person you are caring for.

If You Knew

What if you knew you'd be the last
to touch someone?

If you were taking tickets, for example,
at the theater, tearing them,
giving back the ragged stubs,
you might take care to touch that palm,
brush your fingertips
along the life line's crease.

When a man pulls his wheeled suitcase
too slowly through the airport, when
the car in front of me doesn't signal,
when the clerk at the pharmacy
won't say *Thank you*, I don't remember
they're going to die.

A friend told me she'd been with her aunt.
They'd just had lunch and the waiter,
a young gay man with plum black eyes,
joked as he served the coffee, kissed
her aunt's powdered cheek when they left.
Then they walked half a block and her aunt
dropped dead on the sidewalk.

How close does the dragon's spume
have to come? How wide does the crack
in heaven have to split?
What would people look like

if we could see them as they are,
soaked in honey, stung and swollen,
reckless, pinned against time?

—Ellen Bass, *The Human Line*

BE PRESENT

Being present is an essential art in caring for the dying, and a skill that we can and must learn.

This is where meditation practice comes in. The secret of meditation is very simple—being present. In meditation, we learn to calm down the uncomfortable feeling of inner restlessness, self-criticism and mental distractions, and to stay with *what is*. We learn how to be. Just to be. And by simply being present and doing less, we can come to discover that we often accomplish more.

Mindfulness, awareness, and spaciousness—three key qualities that we cultivate in meditation training—are essential to good care. Mindfulness helps us to stay focused and undistracted without becoming fixated on whatever we are focusing on. Awareness enables us to keep in mind the big picture without losing the details. We become aware of our own feelings, which stops us from projecting them outwardly. The third key quality of meditation, spaciously remaining, gives us stability and a healthy sense of feeling grounded, which makes us less speedy, more open, and more kind.

We can sometimes feel plagued by thoughts that we are not good enough, which makes being present for another extra challenging. We fear being vulnerable and set extremely high expectations for ourselves. In a workshop I gave for young physicians at a large hospital several years ago, some shared stories about the internal pressure they carried from burying their own emotions while caring for a dying patient. "It is often easier to feign compassion and listening rather than to show up." Another resident added, "I'm always thinking about what I have to do next, so I'm never really fully there in the moment." After a long pause, a young doctor ventured, "It is tough just to *be* when you don't know what to *say*." As many of the other group members nodded, he continued, "It's hard to allow myself to forgive and accept how I am. Being in the medical profession, it is common to never accept who you are, and try to be 'better.'" Through this workshop, these young physicians had a chance to identify their coping strategies and to experience the benefits of meditation and mindfulness practice to their approach to care and how to be present.

Meditation training encourages us to make friends with ourselves and be gentler. It is not about acquiring anything new that we did not have before, but about getting in touch with what has been there all along—and what we may have lost touch with: our inner capacity to be present, open, and awake.

When we are at ease with ourselves and able to rest in our caring and authentic presence, people around us can feel that. It naturally strengthens our confidence and capacity to hold space for others' experiences.

Angela works as a pediatrician in palliative care and is a graduate of the Authentic Presence course on the contemplative approach to caring for the dying. "I was astounded when I realized that being present is actually a skill that I can learn and practice," she shared with her group. "My meditation practice has helped me to gently befriend myself and accept my feelings. I am learning to show up in these extremely painful situations because I am more in touch with myself. Believe me, these situations have not become any easier, just more workable."

> We can make our minds so like still water that beings
> gather about us that they may see, it may be, their own
> images, and so live for a moment with a clearer, perhaps
> even with a fiercer life because of our quiet.
> —W. B. Yeats, *The Celtic Twilight*

A common and simple meditation method is to watch the natural flow of the breath, letting it guide us back to being present. Simply being present with our breathing can be deeply healing. It is also a wonderful thing to do at the bedside with a dying person or grieving family member. Just breathing quietly, sitting together. Our breath is connected to what we can call the movement aspect of our mind. When we watch our breath, we calm and pacify our mind. Just as the car stops, the driver stops. The mind settles. Our hope and fear, and our anxiety, dissolve. There is nothing to fix, nothing to prove. Things are okay just as they are, in this moment.

Here is a simple practice you can do anytime, anywhere, whenever you feel scattered, restless, and distracted. In this meditation, try to keep your eyes open. Keeping the eyes open makes it less likely that you will fall asleep, and, most importantly, it helps you to find a balance between being centered in yourself and staying open to the world around you. The next time you are at the bedside and there is nothing else to do but be present for the person, try watching your breath. Watching the natural flow of the breath is a way of allowing all the scattered aspects of our mind to settle, and to bring our mind home.

WATCHING YOUR BREATH

Keep your back straight and the rest of your body as relaxed as possible. A firm back helps you to stay centered and strong, and at the same time a relaxed body makes you open, soft, and gentle.

Leave your eyes open and allow your gaze to be relaxed and natural.

Now, very lightly bring your attention to the simple fact that you're breathing.

If you can't seem to find your breath, try taking one or two breaths deliberately and then let the breath settle into its natural rhythm.

Be mindful of your breathing, without any attempt to force it or control it.

Whenever you get distracted, that's okay. Just notice, return to the breath, and begin again. This may happen over and over, and that's okay too.

Be mindful of your breath, and at the same time be aware and spacious.

Be aware of your environment, the presence of the other person, and the sound of their breathing. Keep your senses open. Remain spacious and present.

For Presence

Awaken to the mystery of being here
and enter the quiet immensity of your own presence.
Have joy and peace in the temple of your senses.

Receive encouragement when new frontiers beckon.

Respond to the call of your gift and the courage to
follow its path.

Let the flame of anger free you of all falsity.

May warmth of heart keep your presence a flame.

May anxiety never linger about you.

May your outer dignity mirror an inner dignity of
soul.

Take time to celebrate the quiet miracles that seek
no attention.

Be consoled in the secret symmetry of your soul.

May you experience each day as a sacred gift woven
around the heart of wonder.

—John O'Donohue
To Bless the Space between Us

JUST LISTEN

"I don't know what to say!"

This is a common worry, and there is no "right" word
that can magically make a situation better. What can make
the suffering more bearable for those who are struggling
is for them to be able to share the weight of the situation
with another person—to reveal their inner world, thoughts,
and feelings, and to know that they are not alone. Listening

plays a big part in accompanying a dying person. Listening deeply—free of any judgment, agenda, or need to fix things—is one of the most powerful gifts that you can offer.

Thoughts

> There's something dangerous
> In being with good talkers.
>
> The fly's stories of his ancestors
> Don't mean much to the frog.
>
> I can't be the noisy person I am
> If you don't stop talking.
>
> Some people talk so brilliantly
> That we get small and vanish.
>
> The shadows near that Dutch woman
> Tell you that Rembrandt is a good listener.
> —Robert Bly, *Morning Poems*

It's surprising how few people listen well. More often than not, listening is just a gap in which we are waiting for our turn to speak, instead of a precious opportunity to understand the other person better and to allow them to feel heard.

When we truly listen, we know when to speak. Then we speak from a quiet place inside us, and what we say comes from a very different space. Listening to another, we hear ourselves. So do your best to listen to the other person with your whole being. Listen to what is said, and also what remains unsaid. This gives those who have lost their sense of integrity and wholeness the chance to reclaim their inner essence, their sense of strength, meaning, and hope.

Rosamund Oliver, a dear colleague of many years, teaches deep listening to caregivers. She explains that, quite often, the act of listening *itself* provides a space in which some kind of transformation or inner healing can take place. When you bring awareness to your listening, you may find that you don't have to *do* anything else. This can be such a relief! There is no longer the need to rush to ask questions, offer expert opinions, or resolve the other person's problem.

"Silence has many dimensions," wrote Thomas Merton. "It can be a regression and an escape, a loss of self, or it can be presence, awareness, unification, self-discovery. Negative silence blurs and confuses our identity, and we lapse into daydreams or diffuse anxieties. Positive silence pulls us together and makes us realize who we are, who we might be, and the distance between the two." Being present through the end, we have the opportunity to offer the gift of supportive positive silence that invites people to discover their own way.

Don't be afraid when the other person grows silent. Pauses and silence in a conversation are as important as the words that are spoken. When people are vulnerable and hurt, silence takes on a much deeper meaning. These intimate moments of silence are like invisible threads that magically weave and hold together the truth of what really needs to be expressed. For in silence, one's inner voice has the chance to emerge, and one can relate with greater clarity to others.

We do not always need to use words to communicate confidence and reassurance. Be comfortable when the conversation grows silent, and sit and enjoy each other's company. This can be incredibly meaningful and healing. Likewise, a warm, unafraid glance or gentle touch can say much more than words.

When you come into the room, can you meet my gaze?
—Voice of a dying person

Listening is a form of spiritual hospitality by which you invite strangers to become friends, to get to know their inner selves more fully, and even to dare to be silent with you.

—Henri Nouwen, *Reaching Out*

Listening to another is a spiritual interaction. The way we listen to people, the whole quality of our presence, can make them feel whole and remind them of their sense of purpose and meaning. And this, in turn, gives purpose to our lives.

JUST LISTEN

The moment you recognize that you feel helpless, anxious, or at a loss for the "right thing" to say to make the other person feel okay, simply notice.

Be aware of what is happening for you, without judging your experience.

Simply be aware, breathe, and relax.

Be honest and natural. Quietly acknowledge, "I don't know what to say, but I'll just be here and we can sit together." And then just listen.

If you feel overwhelmed, or helpless, be careful not to interrupt or diminish what the other person is saying because it can be hard to hear.

Stay. Listen. And then listen some more.

BE MINDFUL IN THE
BEGINNING, MIDDLE, AND END

Everything we do has a beginning, middle, and end. But how much mindful awareness do we bring to this process? Before we even begin a task, we are already preoccupied with what comes next. In the middle, we are distracted, spaced-out, or self-absorbed. And at the end, well, we're already rushing off to the next thing. All of this can be a barrier to being a compassionate presence. To bring more mindful awareness to how we offer care to another, and to make what we do meaningful and give it purpose, we can reflect on what we call the "three goods." This three-goods practice is another way we can connect with our intentions and try to stay present in our care, no matter how challenging or uncomfortable it may be.

THE THREE GOODS

Before you begin, take a moment to connect with your good heart, which is open, clear, and kind—the very best part of your being. Then, set a clear intention to be of benefit. That is *good in the beginning*.

Then, whatever happens, try to keep an open, spacious frame of mind and stay connected to your motivation. Stay connected to the very best part of your being and try to relate to the basic goodness and wholeness of others. Whenever you get distracted, just be aware that you are distracted and return to being present, free from concepts, judgments, and assumptions toward yourself and others. That is *good in the middle*.

At the end, let go of holding on to any particular result or outcome, and offer and dedicate any positive benefit from what you have been doing toward the well-being of yourself as the companion and the person you are caring for. You can consider something like this: "May the benefit of my actions, whatever I have said or done, support me to grow in kindness toward myself and others." We can also offer and dedicate situations where we were unskillful. If there was a moment where you wished you had not done or said something, you can make a resolution by thinking, "May I have more awareness in the future and catch myself before I do something similar." We can offer the goodness and power of what we have done to the person we are caring for. "May it help the dying person overcome what is difficult, painful, and unknown."

If you like, you can widen out your good wishes to include others who are in similar circumstances. You can think something like this: "May it touch all those who are hurting or in pain, ill, or dying and who are, like myself, accompanying a dying person. May it help them to be free from pain, fear, or anxiety, ease their suffering, and contribute to their welfare, bringing them peace of mind." That is *good at the end*.

In a nutshell, the three goods are to be kind, open, and clear in the beginning; kind, open, and clear in the middle; and kind, open, and clear at the end.

You can use everyday things to remind you of the three goods. If you are in a hospital, for example, you can use washing your hands at the sanitizer station next to the room at the beginning and end of your visit to remind you to set your motivation for the visit, and to dedicate any positive benefit at the end. Or you can pause for a moment each time you press down the door handle to go in and out of the dying person's room. Or you can use the handshake or touch when you greet and say goodbye to that person to remember good in the beginning, middle, and end.

To slow down, remember to breathe, be present as fully as you can, and just listen; held within the framework of the three goods, these are essentials at the bedside and in our care and communication.

4

Supporting Connections

Mrs. Ping only spoke Mandarin. She had a seventeen-year-old daughter who came to visit every day. During her visits her daughter always stood at the end of her mother's bed and would only sit down next to her dying mother when we encouraged her to do so. The mother and daughter's helplessness and grief about this painful situation were palpable, yet they never spoke a word to each other and avoided physical contact. The social worker and the rest of the staff tried desperately to find ways to connect them and support their saying goodbye. At the time, I was working night shifts, and when the hospital had quieted down I took some time to sit with Mrs. Ping, wishing silently that she and her daughter could find a way to come together.

During one of my nightly visits, the mother sang a Chinese song in a low, tender, and sad voice. The beautiful and simple melody touched me and I started humming along. Over the next few weeks, every time I visited her, she made it her mission to teach me the song. With great patience and stubborn insistence, she taught me the words—every single syllable—correcting me and sometimes scolding me with a playful grimace on her face as she listened to my poor pronunciation. The social worker managed to record her song and, on the morning she died, when the daughter arrived the social worker gave her the tape.

Listening to her mother's voice, the daughter became tearful. As it turned out, the song was an old Chinese folk song from the village in rural China where her mother had come from so many years ago. The song was about the natural beauty of the place, and the longing to go back home. It seemed to encapsulate her mother's life story. In her very own, simple way, her mother was saying goodbye to her through this song. It was the legacy she left behind.

FOCUS ON WHAT IS POSITIVE

One of the biggest fears and anxieties of dying people is that their life has been wasted and that they are going to meet death empty-handed. Leaving a positive legacy behind for her daughter in the form of a beautiful song was Mrs. Ping's way of preparing for death and saying goodbye.

During the person's illness, particularly while she is still well enough to reflect, it can be a tremendous support to focus on what she has accomplished in life.

When we show the dying person that we care about her life and experiences, we make her life meaningful. So how can we help with this?

Show Appreciation

For some, it will be important to feel appreciated for having lived a productive, positive life and to reflect on how they have contributed to their family, their community, or a good cause. Appreciation, however, is not always about how much people have done in their life. There are the inner qualities of people as well—generosity of heart and spirit, kindness, decency, moral integrity. Express what you appreciate about them, these good qualities, their grit and grace. Perhaps they have taught you something that you still cherish. When you do this, be sensitive and responsive to the person's cultural background, values, and social behaviors.

Inspire Joy

Encourage those who are dying to focus their mind and heart on what gives them a sense of joy, comfort, ease, and peace. Explore things that they still enjoy doing, and do these things together with them. It's fine if the experience of doing these things is different than it was when they were healthy.

Create an Inspiring Environment

If you can, arrange for the physical environment at home or in the hospital to be as peaceful as possible. Place inspiring images in clear view of the dying person, or a beautiful plant or flowers that remind one of nature. You can play a selection of music, or inspirational readings or talks that are meaningful to the person.

Wild Geese

You do not have to be good.
You do not have to walk on your knees
For a hundred miles through the desert, repenting.
You only have to let the soft animal of your body
love what it loves.
Tell me about your despair, yours, and I will tell
    you mine.
Meanwhile the world goes on.
Meanwhile the sun and the clear pebbles of the rain
are moving across the landscapes,
over the prairies and the deep trees,
the mountains and the rivers.
Meanwhile the wild geese, high in the clean blue air,
are heading home again.
Whoever you are, no matter how lonely,
the world offers itself to your imagination,
calls to you like the wild geese, harsh and exciting—
over and over announcing your place
in the family of things.

—Mary Oliver, *Wild Geese*

WORKING THROUGH FEAR AND DENIAL

Sometimes people can struggle with extreme fear and anxiety when faced with the reality of their death. Try not to talk them out of it or diminish their experience and feelings in any way. "Don't worry," or "All will be well" can be meaningless phrases to those who feel anxious and frightened. They are dying, and things are, clearly, *not* okay. Sit down next to them. Honestly acknowledge their existential fears and worries when they surface. They are confronted with *the* most challenging and painful experience of their entire lives: the final, uncompromising moment of truth that we all are, without exception, mortal. Who wouldn't be frightened?

Do let them know that they are not alone. Bring them back to the present moment when their mind spins off into uncertainty of what the future may hold and fears about all the things that could go wrong. Remind them that you are there listening. And keep breathing calmly. You can say something like, "It's completely natural to feel frightened and scared. It takes a lot of courage to face the unknown. But know you are not alone, I am here with you." Then hold their hands, listen, and extend your unconditional love to them. Love is the most powerful antidote to fear. Love, as well as your physical presence, offers safety and reassurance.

If the person is in denial about what is happening, do not try to break through the denial. Denial is a crutch to help the person through this painful time. It makes the unbearable a bit more bearable, if even for a short time. For a person to take in the reality of death is, understandably, overwhelming. As a coping strategy, those who are dying may tend to oscillate between talking about their dying while in their next breath talking about getting better. For the caregiver and the family, this kind of behavior can be frustrating and deeply confusing. This going back and forth, or oscillation, like denial, is a coping mechanism that helps the dying to integrate, piece by piece, the fact that they are dying to their world. You can open the conversation in the form of an exploration, saying something like, "I wish you could be healthy again and be around for a long time, but if that's not possible and you were dying, what would be important to you? What would matter most to you during this time?"

If denial continues and becomes a barrier to making crucial decisions, kindly and gently address the fact that death is drawing close. When you ask them to let go of the "crutch" of denial, encourage them to replace it with hope: the hope of your unwavering support and love, and the hope that they matter. Reassure them that they will be physically well cared for and that they have their own inner strength.

With a kind and clear voice you could say something like, "Dad, you are dying. I wish it were otherwise. We will do whatever you need to make you more comfortable. We will make sure you have the best care. No need to worry. We love you. Dad, you have given us so much for which we will always be grateful. During your life, and particularly during the last few weeks, you have shown much courage. We love you and we are here with you *now*."

If your loved one has arrived at a place of acceptance, be supportive, even if you are not there yet yourself. Be careful of expressions that signal that you are not agreeing with your loved one's decisions. A well-meaning "Don't give up!" or "You can beat this!" says more about our discomfort and struggle to be at peace with the situation than the dying person's. It is hard to see those we love suffer and let them go. Try saying something like, "This must be hard for you. How are you with all this?" If you are not ready to talk, honestly acknowledge this, but let them know, you will make time later. "Dad, right now I feel a bit too overwhelmed to talk. Can we talk about this later today, this afternoon?"

ADDRESSING SPIRITUAL MATTERS

When your loved one, friend, or patient has an inner source of refuge and peace, it can tremendously strengthen their sense of belonging, connection, and hopefulness. For some people, nature can be a great source of peace and comfort. For others, it is a sense of belonging to something bigger than themselves, which may or may not be something spiritual or religious.

Sometimes a person's spiritual or religious beliefs, however, instead of being a source of inspiration and solace, can become a source of spiritual distress and pain. Each year, I hold a meditation retreat at the Spiritual Care Center on the west coast of Ireland high above the cliffs overlooking the vast Atlantic Ocean. The view is stunning and immediately settles down your busy mind. During the last retreat, a health-care worker told the story of an elderly Irish man who was so afraid of the fires of hell that he refused to go to sleep. Once the health-care worker realized his source of distress, through much listening and her caring attention, she was able to guide him back to a place where he felt safe, a place where forgiveness and love were possible and he could find rest.

We must address any deeper existential and spiritual matters from day one of someone's illness. How a person understands their illness, and what and why it is happening, greatly affects their sense of wholeness and well-being. A recent study shows that most people living with a life-threatening illness like to talk about their spiritual beliefs with their doctor.

How can we open up the conversation about spirituality,

spiritual beliefs and faith, and end of life? It's a profound subject.

How Can You Help?

- A straightforward way of approaching existential or spiritual matters for those at the end of life might be to ask if there is anything weighing on their minds or hearts. What has sustained them and given them hope throughout their life?

- You can ask them what they consider as their "spiritual home." This is a nonthreatening way of opening the conversation. A spiritual home could be many things: a particular place in nature, church, or community, a ritual, a memory, an image, or an inner feeling that offers hope, solace, safety, and comfort.

- Find out if they wish to connect with a representative of their community in case they are following a particular faith or spiritual tradition, or the hospital or hospice chaplain. A chaplain is there for people in times of crises, whether religious, spiritual, or not. They are trained to listen and offer support in facing difficult questions about life and death and how to cope with illness and loss.

Later in this chapter, you'll find a series of thoughtful questions to explore together with someone who is living with a terminal diagnosis and approaching the last phase of their life. The main thing is to allow the person to talk about their ultimate concerns, about what really matters. This could be anything, really.

Karen Wyatt, a hospice physician and hospice volunteer from Colorado, reflected in a recent conversation, "In my work in hospice I have long thought about those patients who refuse all spiritual care because they are 'not religious' or just not interested. But all people have a spiritual aspect, whether or not they are aware of it or develop that part of themselves. How can care be offered without offending or intruding upon the patient's own beliefs? So for some individuals the ultimate concern might be a religion or a particular practice, but for others it could be anything—even baseball."

If you feel unsure of how to talk about deeper spiritual matters, remember, you don't need to have all the answers. The dying person may put you on the spot by asking what you think will happen at death, or afterward. Of all the questions, how can we possibly answer this one? I recommend—but only if you are asked—that you share honestly your personal thoughts and any open questions you may have about dying and death. Sharing your own individual beliefs, thoughts, and questions is not about converting the other person. In this process of sharing, there is a sense of openness and respect for each other's values and views, however different they might be. Your genuine openness and attention can enable the person to find her own answers within herself.

> We are not human beings having a spiritual experience;
> we are spiritual beings having a human experience.
>
>   (—attributed to Pierre Teilhard de Chardin)

WHEN YOU DON'T KNOW WHAT TO SAY

At some point in our lives, we have all been on the receiving end of so-called well-meaning advice that usually begins with something like "I know how you feel . . ." or "At least . . ." or "It could be worse . . ." or "Don't cry . . ." In truth, we can never fathom how someone really feels. It is rarely helpful to compare one person's experience to another's, or to encourage someone to stop feeling what they are feeling. We have been taught these stock responses and script-like phrases for crisis situations, but then the script ends and we find ourselves at a loss.

Walking alongside the dying, we quickly realize that there is no fixed script or set formula to follow. So if you are questioning whether what you are about to say is going to be helpful or not, ask yourself how it would feel to hear those words if you were in the same situation. In essence, a dying person needs to hear, feel, and be assured of three things: you matter, you are loved, and your wishes and values are respected.

> I think it is not safe to express how I really feel, deep, deep inside. If I would, what if you turn away? What if I end up all alone?
>
> —Voice of a dying person

QUESTIONS TO HELP YOU MAKE A GENUINE CONNECTION

Every dying person has their own life wisdom. Helping the person to discover or reconnect with this life wisdom is incredibly meaningful, rich, and moving, not only for the dying person but for the listener as well.

> Home is not where you live but where they understand you.
>
> —Christian Morgenstern

Asking good questions can help you to reach out to the dying person, and will make it easier for the person to open up to you. Open questions are generally better; closed questions that prompt a simple yes or no answer often diminish the potential for communication. Open questions encourage the other person to reflect, and give the signal that we are listening.

The following questions have been helpful in encouraging meaningful conversations with the dying. The first set of questions can help open up a conversation. The following sets are arranged around Christine Longaker's "four tasks of living and dying" that were discussed earlier. These are just suggestions and are not meant to be used like a checklist that you have to hurry through and tick off. It might even be helpful just to stick to one question each visit to draw the person out.

Keep in mind that the purpose of these questions is not to enable you to give the other person your own answers. Follow the other's lead and explore what is upmost in their mind. Allow for spaces of silence, be patient, and resist the temptation to jump in. If the urge is too strong, take three long, deep breaths before you respond.

Openers

- Is there anything weighing on your mind or heart that you would like to talk about?
- If there ever comes a time when you want to talk about something or feel frightened, please know that you can always do that.

Understanding and Transforming Suffering

- Are you frightened of dying?
- What do you make of everything that is happening to you?
- What are your fears and concerns? What are your hopes?
- When you went through difficulties in the past, what helped you to get through them?
- What part of you is the strongest right now?

Experiencing Authentic Connection and Love

- Where have you felt connection and love?
- Who has been most important to you?
- Where do you belong?
- Who would you like to be *here*?
- Is there anything you would like to share with them? Is there anything that stops you?
- Are you worried about being a burden to others?
- What are your biggest concerns for the people you leave behind?
- Who would you like me to call when death draws near?

Finding Meaning in Life

- Tell me about your life.
- What has given you joy? What are you proud of?

- Is there anything you are not at peace with?
- What is most important to you now?
- What do you enjoy doing?
- Is there anything you would like to accomplish with the time you have left?
- How would you like to be remembered?

Finding a Refuge or Source of Peace

- What gives you strength?
- What is your spiritual home?
- Is there a religious or spiritual community that you are connected with, or would like to connect with?
- How at peace are you with what is happening?
- Are there things that would offer you comfort?
- Tell me about places or times in your life that brought you peace.
- At the time of dying, is there anything I could do for you?

The way you choose to use the questions will depend on your relationship with the dying person. For some, a direct question might work well. For others, a more indirect and gentle approach might be best. Remember, the purpose of these questions is to reach out and to open the door. It is fine if you don't get a response. You have let them know that it is safe to talk to you, if they choose, whether now or later.

The reality of the other person lies not in what he reveals to you but in what he cannot reveal to you. Therefore, if you would understand him, listen not to what he says but rather to what he does not say.

—Kahlil Gibran,
The Treasured Writings of Kahlil Gibran

Those who are dying will feel safe and connected when we continue spending time with them and thus show them that they matter. We can help them focus their minds on what still gives them a sense of joy, and recognize and celebrate the good things in their lives and what they have accomplished. When they feel confused, fearful, and lost in the dark, our caring attention can guide them through. Even when we stumble while finding the right words, we will show them that we care by listening, by not shying away from their deeper concerns and questions, and by respecting and trusting their own inner wisdom.

5

Deeper Aspects of Caring

"I've had enough. I am a burden on everyone. How can I go on like this?"

When supporting someone in the final months and weeks of his life, some very tough decisions and moments will arise. The dying person may be extremely anxious, afraid to lose his dignity and control, afraid to die or to die alone, afraid to die in pain, afraid to be kept alive against his will or be a burden to the family and run up huge medical bills.

In our society, we value autonomy, freedom, and productivity. Experiences of illness and death poignantly show us how temporary and, on a deeper level, how illusory these values are. They force us to reflect on the value of life *itself* and open our eyes to the nature and meaning of suffering. *What constitutes a meaningful life? What constitutes a dignified death? Has suffering any meaning and purpose? Who am I, when I am no longer in control? Who makes the decisions?*

It is extremely important to discuss these matters early on with the dying person and family members, without judgment, in order to bring hidden fears and concerns out of the shadows before the decision-making becomes an urgent matter. A dying person who feels a loss of dignity is much more likely to experience increased pain, decreased quality of life, isolation, and loss of will to live.

Deeper aspects of caring must honor the dying person's wishes and dignity. This honoring includes supporting the dying person in healing broken relationships and connecting them with a source of refuge when they feel hopeless. Deeper aspects of caring are not solely about the dying person; the concerns of others who are part of the person's journey need to be considered as well.

HONORING THE DYING PERSON'S WISHES AND DIGNITY

Those who are dying may have already made their choices about the kind of care they would like and where and how they would like to spend the end of their lives. In this case, you can help by supporting their choices and simply being present. In other cases, there may still be decisions to make about next steps. You can help them to organize their thoughts about the kind of care they want. Explore with them what they value in life. This will make it easier to understand how they feel about certain choices that they might face when declining health limits their activities and abilities, or when it is clear that their life is approaching its end.

Here is an example of what a friend of mine who works in palliative care wrote in her end-of-life instructions:

"A meaningful life for me would include the ability to recognize and communicate meaningfully with others. Thus, even if I am not necessarily terminally ill, but have brain damage or an impairment that makes me unable to recognize others or be able to communicate with them, then I direct that all life-sustaining treatments be withheld—or if they have been instigated, to be discontinued, even if this results in my death."

This statement made it clear how the writer defined a meaningful life, and that in the absence of these conditions she did not wish to receive any life-sustaining treatment, even if this resulted in her death.

It is crucial that the dying person has a conversation with family members who will be involved in such decisions, to make them aware of his or her values and wishes, and clarify each other's understanding, concerns, and questions. It is ideal that the dying person creates a written health-care directive. Detailed instructions on how to create a directive are beyond the scope of this book, and there are many instructions for preparing these directives online and with legal professionals. There are, however, some helpful questions about meaning and quality of life that some directives miss. The "Resources" section offers you additional considerations to clarify the person's wishes.

If the dying person asks you about the possibility of hastening their death, listen fully and explore the deeper needs behind the request. Likewise, when relatives bring up this question, be present for them. Hearing these thoughts can be very difficult, but they can also reveal helpful information to consider in caring for the dying person. Is there a specific need that has not been met, an underlying fear that has not yet been voiced? Is the fear or concern about something that is actually happening *right now*, or about something that *may* happen in the future? Our natural tendency is to worry about future suffering and pain, which may or may not materialize. This worry can negatively color our present perceptions and experiences. Call on the expertise of your care provider and hospice- and palliative-care services to help you address the dying person's needs and wishes. When we take an honest look at the nature of our fears and concerns, alleviate those concerns, and clarify questions a loved one or patient may have, it will bring both of us back to the present moment. It will create space and, as a result, make it easier to identify all the resources that are available, right here and now, and come up with a plan to put the missing pieces into place.

Whatever ethical or moral dilemma we face, in the end, our action depends on our motivation and on the compassion behind it. In a situation where it is unclear what the person's wishes are, who makes the decisions, or there is a family conflict, emotions tend to run high. Pause and check in the family's point of view. You can use the method of "council" described later in this chapter to create a safe forum for everyone to be heard and listened to. There are no easy answers. In the end, we can only act on whatever wisdom and knowledge is available to us in any given situation.

HEALING RELATIONSHIPS

The dying are particularly vulnerable to regret and guilt. The experience of illness, aging, dying, or grief can bring to the surface intense feelings of blame, anger, or resentment. Unfinished business with a family member, things left unsaid or undone, can weigh heavily on their hearts. When dying people can let go of the emotional pain, they will regain peace of mind, and be able to finally lay down the burden of lacerating guilt or unresolved anger. Knowing the end is near can push them to finally resolve things they have been avoiding for a long time. It can give them the freedom to say things they have never dared to say out loud. As one woman said, "I am dying. This makes it easier to speak my truth."

Joe, a veteran, was from a long line of Irish immigrants. He had a hard life, including a history of addiction and PTSD. Joe had one son, whom he cherished. Joe had walked out on his son's mother when the boy was a teenager, and Joe always felt bad about leaving him behind. Five years later, diagnosed with terminal cancer, Joe gathered his courage and called his son. He left a message on his voicemail to say that he was sorry. His son came to see him the very same day. Joe burst into tears when he saw him walk into his room. He had given up all hope that his son would still care about him after what he had done.

My religion is to live—and die—without regret.

—Milarepa

To offer and accept forgiveness is not always easy. Sometimes the pain of forgiving can feel more acute than the original act that caused the hurt. It might also be mixed in with intense feelings of embarrassment, shame, or guilt. This is true for both the person who is dying as well as the people who love and support that person. Embracing forgiveness, however, does not mean denying or glossing over the painful and difficult things that have happened, or condoning harmful actions. Forgiveness—and this is an important point to convey to a dying person who is struggling to find forgiveness in her heart, either for herself or others, and an important point to remember ourselves—separates the person from her actions. As His Holiness the Dalai Lama has pointed out, "When patience is combined with the ability to discriminate between the action and the one who does it, forgiveness arises naturally."

How Can You Help?

- Listen wholeheartedly to the dying, and allow them to express whatever they are going through freely. After they have expressed their regrets, remind them of their goodness and that they are forgivable.

- Encourage them, if possible, to talk to the person with whom they have unfinished business, and do this in an honest manner and without blame. To help this process, ask them to imagine, if even for a moment, that the other person is truly open and willing to listen to them now. If the person they have unfinished business with is absent, invite them to write a message or record a voice message.

- Remind them that it is okay if there is no resolution. The most important thing is for them to put down the burden of whatever they have been carrying and to have peace of mind.

- If you have unfinished business with the person who is dying, before you go to visit, make sure to take time to reflect on what it is you need to say to them. Check your motivation and frame of mind. This will help to avoid causing further harm. If you find talking helpful, seek out a trusted friend or therapist to clarify your thoughts and feelings. If you find journaling cathartic and clarifying, do that. Any of these processes will support you to put down your burden and be in a better place, even if the other person is unwilling to talk about it or physically no longer able to respond.

Sometimes the resolution we may have supported the dying person to work toward does not arrive as the nice and neat "happy ending" we had wished for. A hospice social worker told the following story. An elderly woman who was dying had not spoken to her daughter in fifteen years, even though the daughter lived only a few miles away. The hospice social worker supported her idea to write a letter. The mother wrote that she was nearing the end of her life and wanted to see her daughter one last time. She also asked her daughter for forgiveness for all the ways she had hurt her. After receiving the letter, the daughter did come to see her mother. But instead of offering her forgiveness, she yelled at her mother for an hour and a half, berating her for all the ways that her mother had wronged her. She then stomped out the door and left. The social worker was appalled at the outcome, but the mother was satisfied. She had asked for forgiveness and offered forgiveness to her daughter—she had done all that she could and found peace with that. She told the upset social worker that it was up to the daughter to determine her own response and that she was able to accept that this was beyond her control.

FINDING A HEART PRACTICE

Whether the dying person has rich relationships, challenging relationships, or few relationships at all, a heart practice can offer solace. If the dying person has a daily practice of meditation or prayer, however brief, encourage them to continue to do it regularly. As the moment of death draws closer, the person's energy will diminish, so it is best to keep it simple. Each person is unique, so there is no one spiritual practice that fits all. You can help the dying person to connect with a ritual or prayer from their own tradition, if they have one, or you might offer a basic practice, such as the ones described earlier in this book. You might also try the Essential Phowa practice described in chapter 8. It's inspired by the Tibetan Buddhist tradition, but is helpful and relevant to people across faith traditions.

How Can You Help?

- Encourage those who are dying to focus on a meditation practice or prayer that they feel they have the strongest heart connection with—one heart practice that embodies all.
- Inspire them to immerse their mind and heart in the peaceful and sacred atmosphere of the practice.
- If the dying person is not familiar with meditation or prayer, and if they are open, gently explore if there is anything that offers them some ease and peace—like repeating a line of prose or poetry, listening to a piece of music, or remembering a moment of deep inspiration, gazing at a beautiful image or the sky outside the window.

The story of my friend Joannie shows how even music can be an important and helpful spiritual practice for someone at the end of life. Joannie was an old hippie at heart. Small, bent over, suffering from multiple ailments, she had a soul that was vibrant and alive. My friends and I often teased her that deep down in the tight enclosed space of her old body was a young girl. One day, she got an infection in her foot that spread rapidly to the rest of her body. She ceased to speak and lapsed into unconsciousness. The prognosis was not good. After days in the intensive care unit and thoughtful conversations among those who loved her, we decided to let her go. She had always been clear that she didn't want heroic measures at the end. The doctors unhooked her from the machines, and the nurse rolled an extra bed into her room, so we could stay overnight. Her friends, her family, and I took turns being with her over the next two days sharing memories from her life. We put small speakers at the head of her bed so she could listen to her favorite mantras, her beloved music from the sixties and seventies, and some jazz pieces mixed in. The night before she died, her friends and family gathered around her bed saying goodbye. There were laughter and tears, and then we stood in silence around her, one last time everyone together. She was unconscious, and as people slowly turned to leave her room, suddenly and without warning, a song came blaring from one of our cell phones. While putting on his jacket, my husband had accidentally hit the button of the music app on his cell phone. It was her favorite song from Santana, a version of "Stairway to Heaven," the song she had gone to sleep with every night for many years. Joannie died peacefully a few hours later, at the first light of dawn.

ACCOMPANYING FAMILY AND FRIENDS

Death does not only touch the person who is ill. It touches everyone around that person. Sometimes, a grieving relative or distressed friend needs attention and loving care. By being present for those who feel anxious and are hurting, we are also supporting the dying person too. That person will have one thing less to worry about.

As someone is dying, powerful family dynamics can be triggered, and old hurts can surface, especially when everyone feels under pressure. Family members may, either openly or behind closed doors, be critical of each other for doing too little or too much, blame each other for not feeling enough or too much, being too attached or not caring enough. Assumptions, expectations, or accusations can block communication and get in the way of making a genuine connection with each other and with the dying person. They affect care and obstruct the process of informed and respectful decision-making. Again, the most important thing is to listen, and help them to listen to each other and find some common ground.

How Can You Help Family or Friends Who Are Hurting?

- Offer those who feel distressed a space to talk, and be generous with your listening. It is best to do this in a separate room, away from other family members and the dying person.
- Reassure them that their sadness or feeling overwhelmed is a normal response to facing the loss of a person they hold dear. Ask them if they have something they would like to tell or express to the dying person.

- Invite them to rehearse what they need to say, with you taking on the role of the dying person, to help them express what they wish to say without such a strong emotional charge or reaction. Encourage them to take some space to settle their emotions before they speak again with other family members and to see the dying person.

- Consider calling a family meeting. A "council" or "talking circle" can be a very effective way to structure a family meeting. It creates a safe environment as each person has the time and space to express what they feel and think without being interrupted. Palliative-care specialist Ann Allegre shared with a group of health-care professionals the power of a talking circle: "While an excellent surgeon relies on their superior surgical instruments, I rely on the talking circle as my most effective tool for supporting the dying and their families." Essentially, in a talking circle, people are invited to sit in a circle, listen in silence, speak from their hearts when it is their turn, and hold space for each other. Everything that is shared remains confidential. The facilitator offers a time frame and a "talking stick"—a stick or a small stone that goes around from person to person—indicating whose turn it is to share. Only the person with the talking stick has permission to speak. In

a traditional council, the talking stick goes around
until everyone has finished speaking.

HOW TO SUPPORT A CHILD WHEN
A LOVED ONE IS DYING

The best advice for speaking to a child when someone is
dying—a beloved grandparent, for example—is to be sensitive
but tell the truth. We may think that by not talking about it,
we are protecting the child from what's happening. This is
not the case. The child will pick up that something is wrong,
not understanding why they get shooed out of a room, or
why we cry. We do not want the child to believe that death
is something strange or terrifying, so we prepare the child
ahead of time when someone they love and know is seriously
ill. Depending on the age, children might already be aware of
death: dead insects on the back porch, a pet rabbit they loved
and that died, the death of their favorite cartoon character,
or the many deaths shown on TV. Even with an awareness
of death, a younger child may not understand that death is
irreversible: "Grandma will be back for my birthday, right?"
Be present for the child as fully and attentively as you can,
just as lovingly as you are with the person who is dying.

Honor the child's good heart by offering them ways to
play a part in the life of the dying person, their parents,

and family members who are grieving. This might include spending time with the child, drawing pictures or letters, reading stories together, or anything that encourages connection. Honestly answer any questions children might ask to help them to make sense of their own experience.

Give them a choice if they want to visit someone who is dying or not. If they are reluctant to be around, find out why. When I was a teenager, my great-grandmother was dying. Her changing skin color, sunken face, and the strange smell of her body frightened me. I felt disgusted, ashamed, and bewildered. I made excuses to avoid visiting her. My grandmother, her daughter, noticed that something was wrong. She sat me down and told me that it is okay not to go unless I wanted to. My great-grandmother knew I loved her. I still remember how relieved I was not to be scolded or guilt-tripped into going. Children can offer love to dying people with their presence or in other ways if it helps them feel more comfortable.

Children may often come to believe that they are in some way responsible for the person's death. It is important to reassure them that this is not their fault, but part of the natural process of life. Having these kinds of talks with a child is not easy and may bring you right back to the time when you lost someone when you were growing up. If you cannot answer all the child's questions, be honest and open about it. Say, "I don't know." Children are resilient, and knowing and feeling they are supported and loved will shape how they approach life and living, death and dying, as adults. Through our actions, we model for them how to reach out to the dying, the bereaved, how to brave dying and death and, ultimately, help them face their own. If we ourselves look upon death as a natural process, so will they. If we allow them to be children, their playfulness and joyfulness can bring much healing to the family.

Last summer, I spent a few weeks at Sukhavati, the first Buddhist center for spiritual care in Germany. Located just an hour outside of Berlin, it enjoys views of an expansive lake and the pale blue skies typical of this region. Open to anyone, Sukhavati offers a space for healing and community, and an environment where seriously ill people can come with their families, either for a short stay or to conclude their lives. Mr. Hans, a father of two young girls, had ALS for some years. Now, he was in the final grip of the illness, locked into his body, and needing twenty-four-hour care. His young wife came to visit almost every day with the girls. They played in the garden outside and moved around the house with an infectious ease and naturalness that painted a smile on everyone's face. When Mr. Hans died, his body, following the wishes of his wife, was laid out in an open casket in the shrine room. While family and friends said their goodbyes and the Protestant minister with whom he was close guided a short service, his daughters played next to the coffin. At the end of the service, each visitor put flowers gathered from the garden on his body. The girls had chosen two bright sunflowers and laid them on their father's chest and then danced, like light-filled fairies, around their mom. Death was visible without it being frightening. There were tears, but life, vibrant and vivacious, continued.

How Can You Help?

- Use simple, clear words appropriate to the child's age and experiences. Be factual: "Grandpa is dying."
- Follow the children's questions. Give them only the information they need at the moment. Pause to check their reactions, before offering more. If they have not asked any questions, you can ask them if they have any. This may elicit sadness, as children tend to have more feelings than thoughts. Then just be with them and respond to their concerns. If they do not have any questions, look fine, and run out to play, let them be. They may need time to process by themselves and in their own ways.
- Use examples from the natural world like seasons changing to show that death is a natural process.
- As children may not have the capacity yet to express their feelings in words, encourage them to share their inner world through art, music, or dance. A child's curiosity, openness, and innocence can actually bring

a sweetness and lightness into the pain of dying, as well as providing a reminder to slow down and be in the present.

- Encourage the child to do something positive for the dying person, to feel that they are really helping.
- Prepare the child for what it's like to be around someone who is dying: for example, that the dying person is getting weaker, may sleep more, does not need to eat or drink anymore, may breathe differently, and that there is nothing to be afraid of. Check how much information the child wants and be aware how much they can process. Ask the hospice team or medical care team to help you explain what's happening.
- Normalize the situation. Ask the child if they want to sit at grandpa's bedside and hold his hand, nap on the couch next to him, sing, or read for a little while. Ask if they can help bring food to the other people visiting or walk the dog.
- After the death has taken place, make sure that you give the child special attention and affection.

It can be helpful to remember that, while the person who has died may not be in a child's life anymore, that person's love is still with them. A hospice nurse witnessed this deeply moving scene. A father dying of lung cancer called his young son to his bedside. He pointed his finger to his son's chest.

"I am in there, you know." The boy sobbed. The father put his hand on the boy's chest. "I will always be there, with you, right here." He gently pressed his big hand on the boy's heart. The boy stopped sobbing and went very quiet. His father kept holding his hand on the boy's chest. After a while, a smile grew on the boy's face. He understood.

Caring for these deeper aspects through the end of life is undoubtedly a big task: making a continued effort to see the dying person in terms of their life, background, values, and history, helping to clear up unfinished business, and being present to a grieving family member, friend, or child. We will not always succeed. Yes, that is true. In those moments when I think I failed and was unaware, I find it helpful to remember that we can never truly know the deeper effects of our care. To be committed to caring for the deeper aspects of another person's life, whether we see any effects from our efforts or not, I believe is in itself a profound and beautiful expression of honoring their life and unique journey.

We also need to remember to include ourselves in the circle of care.

6

Taking Care of Yourself

Taking care of ourselves is not a luxury. It is not selfish. It's a must. If you are caring for a loved one, you will find yourself in many roles—caregiver, partner, confident, medical advisor, counselor, house cleaner, chauffeur, social secretary, shopper, cook, to name just a few. If it is your professional role to care for others and you are caring for a child, sick partner, or elderly parent at home at the same time, then you are doing double duty! You may find yourself "sandwiched," caring for both the younger and the older generation at the same time. You will need the stamina of a long-distance runner. We cannot pour from an empty cup, and if at any point you feel you have reached the edge of your patience and lost any sense of perspective, spaciousness, and humor, then these are warning signs that you have moved beyond your limits and need to pause, breathe, and prioritize care for yourself.

Caring for others requires caring for oneself.
—The Dalai Lama, *Lojong: Training the Mind*

Be kind to yourself as you proceed along this journey. This kindness, in itself, is a means of awakening the spark of love within you and helping others to discover that spark within themselves.

—Tsoknyi Rinpoche, *Open Heart, Open Mind*

BE KIND TO YOURSELF

Compassion is the natural human response to witnessing and experiencing suffering. Our heart goes out to the one who is suffering, and we want to relieve their suffering. Our compassion, however, is not only reserved for others. It begins when we are able to extend the same friendliness, warmth, and understanding that we so readily offer to those we care for, to ourselves.

In a talk to caregivers, Rick Hanson aptly said that "self-compassion applies compassion to the one being . . . who wears our name tag." In being kind to ourselves, we remove the harm and unkindness within us, which in turn allows us to truly care for others. Recent research by Kristin Neff and others demonstrates how self-compassion is not only helping us to muddle through and survive the chaos, turmoil, and stress of difficult times, but to be well, despite it all. Being kind to ourselves makes us resilient and helps us to be well and stay well in the face adversity, and even to grow.

Kindness

Before you know what kindness really is
you must lose things,
feel the future dissolve in a moment
like salt in a weakened broth.
What you held in your hand,
what you counted and carefully saved,
all this must go so you know
how desolate the landscape can be
between the regions of kindness.
How you ride and ride
thinking the bus will never stop,
the passengers eating maize and chicken
will stare out the window forever.

Before you learn the tender gravity of kindness
you must travel where the Indian in a white poncho
lies dead by the side of the road.
You must see how this could be you,
how he too was someone

who journeyed through the night with plans
and the simple breath that kept him alive.

Before you know kindness as the deepest thing inside,
you must know sorrow as the other deepest thing.
You must wake up with sorrow.
You must speak to it till your voice
catches the thread of all sorrows
and you see the size of the cloth.
Then it is only kindness that makes sense anymore,
only kindness that ties your shoes
and sends you out into the day to gaze at bread,
only kindness that raises its head
from the crowd of the world to say
It is I you have been looking for,
and then goes with you everywhere
like a shadow or a friend.

> —Naomi Shihab Nye,
> *Words under the Words: Selected Poems*

The terms *empathy* and *compassion* are often used inter-
changeably, but, for anyone who is in a caregiving role, it is
actually useful to understand that there is a crucial distinc-
tion between the two.

Empathy is the ability to resonate with others' feelings.
It is the precursor for compassion. When we empathize with

the suffering of another, we literally feel their pain. This is, as the latest neuroscientific research shows, a true experience of suffering. Over time, this kind of empathic distress leads to burnout, and it is something that we need to watch out for. When we get caught up in our own emotional resonance with another's pain and suffering and are exposed to deep suffering, anguish, and trauma for long periods of time, we can lose our own sense of well-being.

Compassion is the warmhearted response to suffering, but, unlike empathy, along with it comes a strong sense of responsibility to relieve suffering. We don't remain at the level of feeling alone. We take action. Compassion is important in care. It lowers our stress level and calms our body. It helps us to find our center again when we have lost our balance. In the vast space of compassion there is greater clarity and discernment. The clarity of compassion, the wisdom that compassion brings, shows us what is truly needed in challenging situations.

I often hear the concern that by acting compassionately, we end up a doormat. This is a very simplistic understanding of the true nature of compassion. Compassion can be both tender and fierce, gentle and firm. Compassion prevents us from getting enmeshed and overidentified with another's pain and suffering, from being vulnerable to exhaustion and negativity. We can tell the difference between ours and another's feelings without becoming indifferent.

A compassionately wise outlook allows us to accept our physical, emotional, and mental limits. We come to understand that there are deeper layers and causes to a person's suffering that we may never be able to touch and relieve, however hard we try. Rather than becoming discouraged or depressed by this harsh reality, in the face of suffering, compassion gives us the strength of heart and mind to carry on.

Research shows that the cultivation of compassion can transform and heal empathic distress, the negative side effects of empathy. Research also suggests that it is not compassion that fatigues or wears us out, but empathy. Empathy can lead to negative states of mind, whereas compassion produces positive mental states. The power of compassion can prevent empathic concern from turning into empathic distress.

So, what we commonly refer to as "compassion fatigue," or secondary traumatic stress, sometimes called the "the cost of caring"—which includes symptoms of physical and emotional exhaustion and a profound decrease in the ability to empathize—may actually be "empathic distress fatigue."

Without empathy, we would not be aware of suffering, aware of how someone else feels. We do need empathy to kickstart compassion, but empathy needs to be held by the wisdom, warmhearted tenderness, and strength of compassion.

By cultivating compassion, with the support of the practices described in this book, we are actively strengthening a powerful antidote to the stress of caregiving.

> If a warm, tender heart is not at the core of our compassion, then our sense of responsibility can feel more like a burden that weighs us down without benefiting anyone else.
> —Dzigar Kongtrul Rinpoche, *Training in Tenderness*

It is quite a process to learn to be levelheaded and humble about where we are at personally—that is, to develop an awareness of our strengths as well as our limits. We need to be realistic about what it is that we can offer or do, and at the same time to work compassionately, gently, and skillfully with what we still need to learn and understand. Caring for another, despite our best intentions, we can come to see how we, again and again, get caught in the same habitual patterns and dynamics. We may overcommit ourselves, struggle to say no, be too self-reliant believing we should be able to carry all the burdens single-handedly, or be overbearing in our care. Please don't lose heart. Changing ourselves is a process that takes time and, yes, much patience. Intellectually, we all know this well, but it is often hard to practice, isn't it? I appreciate the following poem that describes the gradual journey of working with and transforming our habits.

Autobiography in Five Short Chapters

Chapter One

I walk down the street.
There is a deep hole in the sidewalk.
I fall in.
I am lost . . . I am hopeless.
It isn't my fault.
It takes forever to find a way out.

Chapter Two

I walk down the same street.
There is a deep hole in the sidewalk.
I pretend I don't see it.
I fall in again.
I can't believe I'm in the same place.
But it isn't my fault.
It still takes a long time to get out.

Chapter Three

I walk down the same street.
There is a deep hole in the sidewalk
I see it is there.
I still fall in . . . it's a habit . . . but,
my eyes are open
I know where I am.

It is *my* fault.
I get out immediately.

Chapter Four
I walk down the same street.
There is a deep hole in the sidewalk
I walk around it.

Chapter Five
I walk down another street.

—Portia Nelson, *There's a Hole in My Sidewalk:
The Romance of Self-Discovery*

Even as we work to understand and change our habits, remember that we—by being just who we are—can offer much benefit and love to someone at the end of life. Extend compassion to yourself. Remind yourself that this is hard, and you are doing the best you can.

When possible, make the time to do some of the things that would usually rejuvenate you, like a walk in nature, a chat with a friend, or an exercise class. If you don't have time for these, you can still be kind to yourself and give yourself the compassion that you need, right now. It is always possible to practice kindness *in the present moment*. Kindness then goes with you everywhere, like a friend.

LOVING-KINDNESS FOR YOURSELF

Pause, breathe, feel your body and the warmth around your heart, and simply be aware.

Just taking this short moment may already feel like a mini break.

If you feel sad, tired, or exhausted, send loving-kindness to your whole being. Consider silently repeating these simple but powerful phrases:

May I be happy, may I be well.
May I be happy, may I be well, and may I be safe.

If you are at a loss as to how to help another and are feeling distressed as a result, consider wholeheartedly sending them loving-kindness.

May you be well, may you be happy, and may you be safe.

GIVE YOUR SADNESS SPACE

Grief does not only start when the dying person is gone. It begins with a terminal diagnosis. We grieve for the life that we knew and the loss of the future that will never be. We begin to imagine what life will be like without our loved one. This is called "anticipatory grief" and is another important reason why we need to be particularly kind and spacious with ourselves. During this time, we can experience sadness and feel tearful, anxious, or depressed; and we can have feelings of loneliness, guilt, anger, fear, or fatigue. We can feel emotionally numb or experience poor concentration and become forgetful.

Separation

Your absence has gone through me
Like thread through a needle.
Everything I do is stitched with its color.
            —W. S. Merwin, *The Second Four Books of Poems*

It is not only the people closest to the dying person who go through these feelings and emotions. Try to acknowledge these feelings as a natural part of the process. Besides good nutrition and sleep, find someone you can share your thoughts and feelings with, whether a friend, a mentor, a therapist, or a spiritual counselor. And keep extending compassion to yourself.

The following practice can offer solace when you are

feeling alone with a heavy heart. You can try it when you have only a few moments to reflect, or you can sit with it for a longer time, extending loving compassion to yourself as you extend compassion to others.

BEING A FRIEND TO YOURSELF

Imagine embracing yourself like a true friend would.

Consider that you are breathing in whatever weighs heavily on your heart, body, and spirit, and breathing out warmth, love, and reassurance to yourself.

Breathe in whatever is troubling you, and breathe out calm, clarity, and acceptance.

While doing this you can acknowledge the part of you that is grieving, afraid of the loss, and fearful of what the future might hold.

Like a loving friend, extend compassion and understanding toward this suffering.

With each out breath, consider that the part of you that is struggling fully receives the love and friendship that you extend to it, and allow yourself to rest in that feeling.

At the end, let go of working with the breath and simply rest in the feeling, the atmosphere of compassion for yourself, for a couple of breaths, or longer.

IT IS NOTHING PERSONAL

Those who are dying may refuse your help. If this happens, do let them know that you heard them and respect their wishes, and offer to come back later to check back in again. If they continue to refuse your help, exhibit strong emotions such as anger, or start to blame you or others, it is hard not to take it personally. Muster all your strength, courage, and love. When those who are dying are overwhelmed or feel embittered by their experience and unable to cope, they may lash out, and their suffering can spill over onto those around them.

Whenever their behavior is upsetting, instead of judging, try to understand. I know it can feel deeply personal. How can it not feel personal when someone is angry with us and lashes out? Especially when we are trying to help? In my experience, the moment I get hooked by someone's emotional outburst, I lose my equanimity. This hurts me and is not helpful to the other person. In order to de-escalate this dynamic, I need to keep my seat: come back to my ground again, try to see and relate to the person's basic goodness, and remain stable and confident. The following practice can help prevent getting caught up in emotional reactivity. Step away from the situation, if you can, to pause and reflect more deeply, or keep the following ideas in mind as you continue to be in the person's presence. In a charged moment, you may also find it useful to return to one of the practices from chapters 2 and 3, which can help you find your breath and stay present in the moment and in your body, rather than being swept away in your own strong emotions.

RECOGNIZING OTHERS' GOODNESS

In the midst of confusion, strong emotions, or negativity, shift your awareness to the inherent goodness or best part of that person, the part that is capable of being open, loving, and clear—however clouded it may appear at that moment.

Try to understand the pain and the deep grief and fear underneath the behavior you see, and acknowledge what is going on: that person is losing their entire world, including everything they hold dear.

Ask yourself: Do I have an inkling of how that must feel?

If you find yourself in an emotionally charged situation, try to maintain your equanimity and not react in a way that might be harmful or cause you to feel regret later.

Imagine that you are a mountain, steadfast and unshakeable. A mountain is never affected by a storm, no matter how strong the winds swirling around it might be.

KEEP YOUR SENSE OF HUMOR

"Are you dead yet?" a high-pitched voice echoed across the room. "Are you dead yet . . . *you* in the corner?" Amanda, an old lady with tufts of white hair who had lived all her life on the streets before being admitted to hospice, was ill-tempered and moody. Thinking she was asleep, I was sitting in silence, but she had in fact been watching me out of the corner of her eye. "Annoying, huh? Having a corpse like me sitting here?" I responded to my surprise. "Yeah!" she growled back with a big grin. "Dead people don't do it for me." I had to chuckle. "Me neither!" I laughed. Amanda grinned again, exposing her missing front teeth. She had found a friend. And she also showed how connecting and healing a moment of levity can be.

A common myth is that humor is inappropriate at the deathbed. In fact, the degree to which we are able to display humor is actually a healthy measure of our well-being as a companion. As long as it is not sarcasm or cynicism, humor is not hurtful. Humor comes from a place of kinship and understanding, and it can help to create some space where there is none. Lighthearted humor, used skillfully, gently, and respectfully, can bring some much-needed ordinariness, warmth, and richness into an already intense situation. More often than not, the main challenge for us as companions is to get ourselves out of the way, by letting go of our own agenda and expectations. When we treat dying as a solemn and serious affair, this will stifle any sense of aliveness, spontaneity, and joy. As a result, we can come to view the dying person as a helpless victim, and what we offer, the act of caring, becomes a burden.

Dying can be messy. Every so often, while trying your absolute best, you may find yourself in an absurdly ridiculous, if not funny, situation in which you cannot help but laugh out loud. With humor, our shared human experience of living and dying becomes more bearable. Sometimes it is the wit of the dying person that lightens up what can be an otherwise emotionally charged situation. One of my colleagues was caring for an elderly gentleman. As his death drew near, he kept gesturing with his frail hands toward the ceiling saying, "Light! Light!" His concerned care team thought he was seeing *the* light, a visual experience that can happen in the final process of dying and that for many is greatly comforting. The gentleman, however, was not referring to any kind of spiritual experience but, as it turned out, he was simply bothered by the glaring overhead light!

Ryan, a chaplain, recounted in one of my workshops a humorous story about a time when he was caring for a young woman. She had spent most of her life working on a farm in upstate New York and had a good and practical head on her shoulders. When it came down to the nitty-gritty details of getting ready for the end, he asked the woman what she wanted to wear after her death. "Well how should I know?" she responded, slightly annoyed. "I don't know what the weather will be like on that day!"

ALLOW OTHERS TO SUPPORT YOU

Caring is best done in a community. We are all part of intricate and dynamic relationships that make up our lives. During the last months and weeks of someone's life, these different relationships can turn into circles of care surrounding the dying person, with an inner circle of core supporters and widening circles around them.

Besides the support from medical providers, hospice, and palliative care, ask friends, neighbors, or members of the person's spiritual community for help, and allow them to help you, because no one can do this alone. You may be surprised who steps forward. People may have held back, unsure of whether they were welcome or would be intruding during this intimate and precious time. Perhaps all they need is an invitation, the offer of a place in the circles of care. If it is too much for you to organize, ask someone else to help you organize the support that is needed, such as grocery shopping, checking the mail, or scheduling visits. Asking for help is not a sign of weakness or an admission that we have failed. It shows, in fact, that we are mature and wise enough to know our limits.

We all have different capacities and talents. Some people are good listeners; others are great at the many practical things that need to be taken care of. Accompanying a person with a terminal illness is not just sitting at their bedside. There are lots of ordinary tasks to be done: paperwork, changing sheets, making tea, shopping, organizing visitors, shuttling the person back and forth to various medical appointments, and so on. Taking care of these seemingly ordinary tasks is an expression of care. The key question is *how* we do these ordinary tasks—the frame of mind we bring to them, and whether we are inspired by mindful awareness and deep care.

Nature can inspire us with an understanding of care in community. Late in October, thousands of cranes gather around the wetlands near Sukhavati Spiritual Care Center. The elegant birds with their long beaks fill the skies, and their cries, like trumpets, can be heard from far away. In the hundreds and in orderly V formations, they fly over the dark land that is getting ready for the long winter. At sunset, if you catch just the right moment to look up when they fly over your head, it is as if you can touch them, and, elated by their presence, majestic and powerful, you feel as if you fly with them. The old or sick birds fly in the back escorted by two fellow birds on either side so they don't get lost in the dark. Isn't this what we do when caring for a dying friend or loved one? In community and with others' support, we take care of those who are most vulnerable.

Caring for another can have many rewards. It can make us feel good, and our life meaningful. Rest in these positive feelings. This is a crucial point. These positive feelings will nourish and sustain you. These states of well-being and purpose are different from a sense of pride that sometimes gets in the way. Pride is one of ego's many traps. It makes us believe that "only we know best." With this kind of attitude, inevitably we end up having unrealistic expectations of ourselves. We grow resentful, frustrated, and overly critical of others because they do not meet our high standards, or they do things differently. Working together to support the dying person, it is good to remember that while others may not do things in the same way that you would, they are still doing their best.

Try to soften and open your heart by recalling a moment when someone was kind to you. Bring to mind how it made you feel. This will help you cut through experiences of isolation at those times when you think that a situation or certain people are unfair and all you can see is others' shortcomings. This will allow you to step back into and feel part of the supportive circle of care again, and see that you are not independent, but interdependent with others.

The following practice, "Unsealing the Spring," can be immensely helpful in sitting with kindness—especially the kindness we've received. Try this practice any time you are feeling like your spirit needs nourishment, when you are feeling challenged to persist, or if you are feeling frustrated in your relationships with other caregivers. You can try the practice in a couple of minutes, or you can sit with these reflections for a longer time to more fully experience the unfolding of love and gratitude.

UNSEALING THE SPRING

Cast your mind back to a time when you received a gesture of love or act of kindness from someone that really moved you. Perhaps it was in your childhood, from your grandmother or grandfather, a mentor, or friend.

Recreate this moment when someone was deeply kind to you, and you felt that person's kindness and love vividly. Almost visualize how it happened.

Now let that feeling arise again in your heart and infuse you with gratitude.

As you do so, allow these feelings of warmth, gratitude, kindness, and love to flow naturally back to the person who evoked them.

Let your heart open, and let kindness and love flow from it.

Then, extend these feelings to others, beginning with those who are closest to you.

Next, extend your love to friends, acquaintances, neighbors, strangers, and even to those you don't like, people with whom you have difficulties.

Let these feelings of warmth, connectedness, and love become more and more boundless.

EMBRACING FORGIVENESS

In our role as a caregiver, at times we can feel stretched to the breaking point—especially within our family. We find ourselves losing our patience, not being as skillful as we wish to be, putting unrealistic expectations on ourselves, and judging ourselves for not being able to do more. Whenever you make a mistake in your interactions or think you have failed, don't beat yourself up. Simply recognize when you have been unable to be skillful or kind, acknowledge it, rekindle your compassionate motivation, and start afresh. Trust in your good heart and your genuine wish to help and extend compassion toward yourself.

> Forgiveness is the name of love practiced among people who love poorly. The hard truth is that all people love poorly. We need to forgive and be forgiven every day, every hour increasingly. That is the great work of love among the fellowship of the weak that is the human family.
>
> —Henri Nouwen

There is so much need for forgiveness and understanding in our lives, and more so at the time when someone is dying. We are all imperfect and vulnerable, and we are all fundamentally good and whole. This provides the ground for us to care for those whom we accompany.

Earlier in the book we looked at how to help those who are dying heal the challenging relationships in their life. As caregivers, friends, and family we also have our work to do. We need to forgive ourselves, and we may also need to work toward forgiveness for the person we are caring for. Even if you can't find full forgiveness, addressing the challenges and talking directly with each other can help both of you move toward healing. If you are caring for a relative or friend with whom you have unfinished business, try to talk to the dying person while they are still well enough. Honestly acknowledge what you feel has been a difficulty, burden, or strain on the relationship, without a sense of blame. Make sure you also express the positive things that you have shared together and, if you can find it in your heart, forgive and express your love. If the person is too ill to talk with, make time to write down your thoughts and feelings in your journal to reach a place of calm and forgiveness within yourself. You can also talk with a trusted friend or a counselor to help you through this process. Then, when you feel ready, even if the person is unresponsive, you can sit quietly at their bedside and express what you need to say; express the difficulties as well as the good things you have shared together. Even if you are not ready to forgive or offer forgiveness, you can consider holding the intention of forgiveness.

You can try the following practice whenever you feel you have acted unskillfully, or there are things you have said or done that you deeply regret. These can be large, life conflicts, or small challenges in the course of care. This practice can be helpful in forgiving yourself, and it can also be helpful in extending forgiveness to others.

SELF-FORGIVENESS AND RECONCILIATION

Begin by connecting first with the best part of your being that is open, clear, and caring. Trust and feel that this part of your being holds with great kindness the part of yourself that acted unskillfully.

Use your breath to work with extending forgiveness to yourself. As you breathe in, consider that you accept total responsibility for your actions and any blame, without justifying or defending yourself. Imagine breathing in any tension with each in breath.

Then, with each out breath, extend forgiveness to yourself for anything you have said or done that was unskillful or hurtful.

Breathe in any negativity or criticism, and breathe out forgiveness.

Then, offer reconciliation and forgiveness to the other person. Consider that you are breathing in misunderstanding, frustration, or any old grudges, and breathing out respect, tolerance, and understanding.

When we are caring for a dying person and caring for ourselves, staying well within ourselves is an ongoing balancing act. Sometimes we are steady, and there are other times when we lose our balance and fall over the edge. This is human. Don't lose heart. There are many resources available to us to heal our own wounds and help us feel supported. Be with others who understand you, and you can share honestly about how you are. Allow others to support you. Try one of the self-compassion practices offered in this chapter that you connect with, whether it's Being a Friend to Yourself, Loving-Kindness for Yourself, Self-Forgiveness and Reconciliation, or Unsealing the Spring. Stay with the practice and let it nourish you, especially when you don't feel like doing it or think that nothing could help. Even if you can do the practice for just a short time each day— say, five to ten minutes as you start your day or "on the spot" when you most need it—it will make a difference. At times when things are just too stressful, it is about placing one foot in front of the other. Breathe. And continue to be kind to yourself as you take each step along your journey of caring for another.

7

When Death Approaches

Sam was a young man in his midthirties. He was dying of cancer. As his end drew near, his body would go into spasms. His family was in agony and distress watching him die in this way. A number of us from his care team tried to soothe him by gently holding him. It was a heart-wrenching scene. We all felt his pain and struggle—his family, the entire ward—yet there was always an invisible net of love and connection surrounding him. He did not have to do this alone. You can never really know what a person's inner experience of his dying process is like. Eventually, Sam calmed down, and his body and facial features relaxed right before he took his final breath. There was an incredible sense of stillness and peace in the atmosphere. We continued sitting with him in this special atmosphere, without saying a word, for what felt like a very long time. A few days later, his family came back to pick up his belongings. His mother was in tears. With the help of a Korean translator, she told us that, even though her son had died far too early and his dying had been very difficult to watch, she felt there was a feeling of love present in the room and between the two of them. It was something they had never talked about while he was still alive.

GIVE HAPPINESS, TRANSFORM SUFFERING

When we accompany someone who is nearing death, there are powerful and profound moments when the other person's sorrow and suffering touch us deeply. The protective shell that has been separating us from each other breaks open, and we know and feel that this person's suffering is, in fact, our own. Our heart opens to the suffering in the world and spontaneously goes out to the dying person, and we wish from the core of our being that we could take away the person's pain, if only for a brief instant.

In these powerful and profound moments, we get a glimpse of the strength and transforming force of genuinely selfless compassion. Use these moments; don't brush them off. Allow them to release the heart of your compassion.

Real fearlessness is the product of tenderness. It comes from letting the world tickle your heart, your raw and beautiful heart. You are willing to open up, without resistance or shyness, and face the world. You are willing to share your heart with others.

—Chögyam Trungpa,
Shambhala: The Sacred Path of the Warrior

Tonglen is one of the most powerful and transformative practices of Tibetan Buddhism. It works directly with the suffering of others and is fueled by the profound wish to relieve it. In the practice—the term *tonglen* means something like "giving and receiving using the breath" or "giving happiness and receiving suffering"—we mentally take on another person's suffering and send that person happiness and peace of mind. Doing the practice won't in any way harm us. Tonglen unblocks the healing energies of our mind and heart by diminishing and ultimately removing our self-absorption and self-centeredness, which are the biggest obstacles to being in touch with our good heart and expressing and embodying our basic human qualities of kindness and compassion.

It is certainly a big leap to work with others' suffering directly in this way. So, before you try it out, make sure that you first strengthen the qualities of fearless compassion within yourself; familiarity with the practices described in chapter 6, including Loving-Kindness for Yourself, Self-Forgiveness and Reconciliation, Being a Friend to Yourself, and Unsealing the Spring, will help. As caregivers, we can be so focused on the other person that we can easily neglect these steps in preparing ourselves to give compassionate care. But if we don't learn to be self-compassionate and take the time to be a good friend to ourselves, inevitably we will end up neglecting our own needs and overextending ourselves until we reach a breaking point. We might also use what we do as a way of escaping our own fears and distress and avoiding our own vulnerability. The tonglen method of mentally taking in others' suffering with fearless compassion, using the medium of our breath, requires that we hold ourselves with the same unconditional acceptance and love that we wish to offer to others.

This is a practice that can be done at any point in a person's illness, and it can be particularly powerful as the end of life approaches. You can do this practice at the bedside, or from a distance.

TONGLEN

Before you begin, take a moment to sit quietly and connect with your compassionate motivation.

To open up the practice, you can begin by considering the person you are practicing for as being the same as yourself.

Then, become aware of the different aspects of the person's

suffering and pain, and allow that person's experience to touch you and open your heart.

Then, as your heart opens, with a feeling of deep compassion, consider that you are breathing in the suffering of that person.

As you breathe out, with love, consider that you are breathing out well-being and happiness to that person.

If you wish, you can deepen your meditation further by imagining that the person's suffering takes on the form of a dark cloud.

As you breathe in the dark cloud, it is transformed at your heart center. Consider that this process of transformation destroys any traces of self-centeredness, small-mindedness, and fear, and strengthens and reveals your compassionate heart more and more.

And, as you breathe out with a feeling of love, imagine that you are breathing out white, cooling light to the person who is experiencing suffering, sending whatever they most need— ease, freedom from pain, relaxation, peace of mind, happiness, acceptance, forgiveness, love, and ultimate well-being.

Breathe naturally, in and out, as you continue with the practice.

If you feel any hesitation about doing the tonglen practice, you can imagine yourself doing the practice, saying in your mind, "May I be able to take on the suffering of others;

may I be able to give my well-being and happiness to them." Simply doing this will help create the climate in your mind that could inspire you to begin practicing tonglen directly in the future.

EXPRESSING YOUR LOVE
AND SAYING GOODBYE

It is not just the one that is dying who has to let go and say goodbye, but everyone close to that person as well. One of the great achievements of the hospice movement is to make more widely known how important it is to help the whole family face their own grief and insecurity about the future. Some people may feel that letting go is a betrayal and a sign that they do not love the dying person enough. Invite family members to imagine that they are in the place of the one who is dying and would have no choice about leaving: How would they want the people they love to be saying goodbye to them? What would help them most on their journey?

Even a simple reflection like this can help so much in enabling someone close to the dying person to deal with the sadness of saying goodbye.

End-of-life care holds to the noble principle that nobody should die alone. Many dying people, however, seem to choose to die alone, when their loved ones who have been at their side for days briefly step out of the room. If this happens, don't blame yourself. Out of love, it might have been easier for the dying person to let go in this way.

Sometimes those who are dying can linger on, and experience prolonged suffering as a result. You can help by giving them your permission to let go. Reassure them with the deepest and most sincere tenderness that those who are left behind will be all right after they are gone. With tenderness and love you can say something like this:

> I am here with you and I love you. You are dying, and that is completely natural; it happens to everyone. I wish you could stay here with me, but I don't want you to suffer any more. The time we have had together has been enough, and I shall always cherish it. Please now don't hold on to life any longer. Let go. I give you my full and heartfelt permission to die. You are not alone, now or ever. You have all my love.
>
> —*The Tibetan Book of Living and Dying*

CREATING SACRED SPACE

The space in which a person dies is of great importance. Space is not just a matter of the physical environment of the person's room, the interior design, or inspiring things on the nightstand, for example, as discussed earlier. Closer to the end, what is equally—if not more—important is the inner spiritual awareness we bring to the bedside and that holds space for the person, recognizing and honoring the moment of death as sacred.

How Can You Help?

- Remind the doctor and staff that you would like to be informed when death is imminent. When death is near, you might request the following:

  Please help us to arrange to bring my loved one home to die, or at least move him to a private room.

  Please disconnect all monitors and discontinue all injections, IVs, tests, or other procedures that are not needed for comfort care.

  When it is clear that my loved one is dying, please do not attempt resuscitation.

- At the moment of death and immediately after someone has died, remain calm and, as much as possible, maintain a peaceful atmosphere in the room. If you feel overcome by emotions, steady yourself by doing the practice of Finding a Place of Calm (chapter 2) and then do the practice of Essential Phowa (chapter 8) or send loving-kindness to the person who has died (chapter 6). Focusing your mind on any of the "on-the-spot practices," if even for a short while, will help you feel more centered and stable.

- Ask family and friends who are present to support the peaceful atmosphere and, if they can, sit with the person, and quietly say their goodbyes. Some may think that death cut them off from the opportunity to communicate one final time and that they missed this precious chance, which can deepen their grief and despair. Yet, there is always the opportunity to express one's love, especially right after death. In the Tibetan Buddhist tradition, unlike the perspective of modern medicine, death is seen as an internal process that still continues after the person has taken their last breath and all the vital signs are gone. This process, of course, varies, but is believed to take up to twenty minutes. Whether you believe this or not, right after death can still be a precious time to share your thoughts with the person who has passed away.

- Encourage people to do their own prayers or meditation, if they wish. To pray for those who are dying or have died can simply mean to wish that whatever suffering they have gone through is over, and lasting peace is theirs.

- You can offer your own prayers or practices at this time, such as the practice of Essential Phowa described in chapter 8.
- Allow those close to the person space to grieve and to let go. If they are emotionally distraught, it might be best to sit with them in another room and listen to them, until they are ready to be with the dying person.

AFTER THE DEATH

If it is clear that the person is going to pass away in a hospital or nursing home, you can request permission ahead of time for the body to be left undisturbed for a few hours after death, so that you have time to sit with your loved one. Sometimes, it may even be possible for the body to be left undisturbed for twenty-four hours. When informed about the special wishes of the deceased, hospital staff may be sympathetic to your request.

In case a death takes place at home and is expected, with hospice or a physician involved, you do not need to call the funeral home straight away to arrange for the body to be removed. An expected death is not an emergency. If you wish, you can keep the body at home for a couple of hours, or a day, or longer. The length of time a body may remain at home varies from state to state in the United States, but may also depend on your level of comfort. People have different levels of comfort being around a body, and that is okay. There are many different ways to respect the sanctity of the body and honor the memory of the person. The hospice team can tell you more about this, help you think through your wishes, and prepare ahead of time so there are no surprises.

Holding vigil has been practiced in many cultures throughout the centuries, though it seems to be almost lost in the Western world. In rural Ireland, in small villages, people still practice having a wake. If you asked, some would say it is just another excuse to have a drink or two. But, there is a deeper communal and spiritual aspect to it. One Irish writer described a wake as a place and time where the living, the bereaved, and the dead remain bound together. *Mná caointe*—the wailing women—watch over the process of dying, praying and keening. After death, the body is laid out in the main room. The entire community comes, even strangers, to wake through the day and night: to pray, exchange the latest news in the village, and be with the grieving family. In the westernmost part of the island, facing the stormy Atlantic, the local radio station announces daily the deaths, including the funeral arrangements, in case one hasn't heard yet.

When my dear friend John died of AIDS, he had his very own version of an Irish wake. We laid him out in a coffin made out of cardboard that had come from a local alternative funeral home. We kept his body cool with dry ice, and we ordered his favorite food and drinks from a shopping list he had written down in advance and meant for this occasion. He knew so many people. And they all came. People cried and laughed through their tears. They said their goodbyes, left written messages, poems, and drawn pictures, and glued the knickknacks he loved so much onto the cardboard box. In the evening, his body was enshrined in what looked like a brightly colored sparkling jewel box filled with all the treasures of his short, but well-lived, life.

A wake, a memorial service, or any kind of ritual that brings people together and helps them to say goodbye can be a wonderful way to celebrate someone's life, honor their memory, and offer spiritual care. Thinking about a wake or service before death might be a challenge emotionally, but it can also be another way to prepare yourself and to honor the life of someone beloved.

HEALING LOSS

How do we heal our brokenheartedness once someone is gone?

In the days, weeks, and months that follow the death, be kind to yourself. Grief needs time to heal, and much caring attention. You may fear that you will not survive your pain and sadness. It may be very difficult to focus and think clearly, or to remember what to do. Don't hesitate to ask a friend or another family member to be with you and support you through all that needs to be done. If you wish, you could practice or pray together for the loved one who has died.

Whatever beliefs you have about what happens after death, when someone close to you dies, it is natural that they remain close in thought. Reminders and memories come, and acknowledging their presence, as well as the loss, is a way of honoring the person's place in your life.

A spiritual practice or ritual can be a source of tremendous consolation and healing when you are grieving, helping to ease the painful feelings of helplessness that can surface. It gives us something concrete that we can do for the person we have lost, and a beautiful and profound way of showing our love and spiritual support.

Often it is only those who have gone through a similar experience who can truly understand our situation and what it really is like. A bereavement group is a safe space to be with our loss without being judged or pressured, a space where we can regain our inner balance through human connections and friendships. You can also seek advice from a counselor who is specialized in grief and bereavement. Naturally, when we face the loss of someone close to us, there are feelings of deep sadness, sorrow, and heartbreak. At times, we need to distract ourselves to be able to cope with the loss. At other times, we may be able to see that the experience is an invitation for reflection, a time to look at our lives and explore a new direction and meaning. As our heart breaks, it can *break open* to the incredible beauty and the vibrant life, love, and richness around us.

Grief needs time to heal, and the healing often takes longer than we expect. Do take the time you need to heal, however long it takes. While writing these lines, a friend shared with me a post from a public online forum. A woman was seeking advice on how to heal her grief over losing a close friend. Many responded. Among the responses was one from an old man. "I wish I could say you get used to people dying. I never did. I don't want to. It tears a hole through me whenever somebody I love dies, no matter the circumstances. But I don't want it to 'not matter.' I don't want it to be something that just passes. My scars are a testament to the love and the relationship that I had for and with that person. And if the scar is deep, so was the love. So be it. Scars are a testament to life. . . . If you're lucky, you'll have lots of scars from lots of loves."

Supporting someone after a loss, we don't want to intrude. We want to give the grieving room. This is important. But human connection and friendship are equally—if not more—important during times of deep sorrow. Be there when the grieving person needs you. Offer your companionship and presence. Help them with the practical details that continue to need attention. Do things they enjoy. Each person grieves and braves loss differently. Be patient with their process. Keep checking in, even if they said that they are fine.

Bearing witness to the realities of the dying process and journeying through grief—these are powerful catalysts to radically transform our hearts and minds. Being a companion and standing at the very threshold of life and death, we have the chance to cultivate fearless compassion— and to enter sacred space.

8

For the Moment of Death and Beyond

Mary had always considered Jesus her spiritual refuge. When she was barely fifty, cancer cut her life short. As death drew near, Mary grew more and more anxious. One evening I was visiting with her. She was visibly upset. "Jesus does not love me. Jesus does not love me," she kept repeating, with tears streaming down her pale face. At the most vulnerable time of her life, she felt utterly bereft of her most important source of strength and refuge. "Mary, Jesus does love you. That is his nature. Jesus loves you," I found myself saying gently to her. "Mary, Jesus loves you."

A few nights later, Mary entered the dying process. I sat at her bedside watching her. I decided to do a silent meditation practice that I find very helpful both for myself and for the dying person as death approaches. I'll describe the practice, called Essential Phowa (pronounced *poh-wa*), in more detail later in the chapter. I visualized an embodiment of wisdom and compassion in radiant, golden light above Mary's bed. Jesus came almost immediately to my mind. I visualized him as a luminous presence in the room. Her breath was labored, and there was a feeling of restlessness hanging over the entire room. As I continued to do the practice, she appeared to grow increasingly more peaceful, and so did the room. At the actual moment of her death, she took three long breaths. "Mary, Jesus loves you," I said softly and slowly. She seemed already so far away, probably unable to hear my words. Yet to my amazement I heard a soft, barely audible "Yes" as she exhaled her final breath. The room was completely silent. An incredible peace enveloped the space. Mary was gone. All I could do was continue to do the practice and be with her, in awe of the mystery of what we call death.

The process of dying and the moment of death are more than just medical events. Being with someone during their last weeks and days is an invitation to enter a sacred space and to bear witness to one of life's greatest mysteries.

Phowa is considered by Tibetan Buddhists to be the most valuable and powerful practice for the moment of death; it's meant to guide and support the transference of consciousness that occurs when a person dies. The practice is an advanced form of meditation that requires detailed instruction and intensive training. The practice I did at Mary's bedside is a simple and universal form of phowa, called Essential Phowa. This is a meditation anyone can do and was first introduced to Western audiences in the classic book *The Tibetan Book of Living and Dying*. We can do the practice of Essential Phowa for ourselves, or we can do it for others.

Essential Phowa creates a calm and peaceful atmosphere that benefits not only the dying person, but also those who care for him or her, whether it be in the intensive care unit, emergency room, hospice, or at home. The beauty of the practice is that it can be adapted to an individual's own beliefs and thoughts, to what resonates and brings a sense of refuge, peace, or comfort. Neither the person offering the practice nor the person receiving it has to subscribe to the Buddhist belief system—or any belief system for that matter—for the practice to be effective. In the practice, you visualize or think of a Buddha, or any other spiritual or religious figure, like Jesus in Mary's case. You can also visualize radiant light. You can make this practice as elaborate or as simple as you like. A common concern is how we should do this practice if we do not know someone's personal beliefs or tradition. What if we do it *wrong*? There is not a wrong way to do this practice. Whether the person we practice for follows a particular religious or spiritual tradition or none at all, we are in no way harming or disrespecting the person's beliefs and convictions.

Essential Phowa is not only a practice for the moment of death, it is also a practice we can do throughout our entire life, when going through a crisis such as ill-health, when facing a loss, or whenever we feel we need support, a space to offer us comfort, safety, peace, and healing.

> Let go of attachment and aversion
> Keep your heart and mind pure;
> Unite your mind with the wisdom mind of the buddhas;
> Rest in the nature of mind.
>
> > —"Heart Advice for the Moment of Death,"
> > from the Tibetan Buddhist Tradition

Essential Phowa is exceptionally supportive when it is time to say goodbye; it can help to mend broken relationships and create the space for that deeper, inner process of discovering or reconnecting with a source of refuge or love. Moreover, this practice can also be done after someone has died as a way of offering our continued spiritual support.

When we first start doing the practice, we may relate to the presence we call upon as something external and distant from ourselves. Consider the presence not as something outside or separate from yourself, but as a reflection of your inner source of wisdom and compassion. Imagine you are evoking and tapping into your own good qualities that have always and reliably been present within you. Visualizing an outer presence of an embodiment of whatever truth we believe in, either in the form of a spiritual figure or radiant light, or simply connecting on a feeling level, can be a skillful method to center ourselves and reconnect and relax back into the core of our being, which is sacred. Christina Puchalski, a physician and pioneer in spirituality and medicine, beautifully illuminates the process of being a compassionate presence to someone who is sick and dying. Compassionate presence, she explains, means connecting to the sacred in another from the sacred place within us.

ESSENTIAL PHOWA FOR YOURSELF

First make sure you are comfortable, with your spine straight and the rest of your body relaxed. Close your eyes and allow your mind to settle. Spend a few moments connecting with your compassionate motivation for doing the practice. During the practice, you can keep your eyes closed, if you wish.

Visualize, as a body of light in the space in front of you or above your head, the embodiment of whatever truth, wisdom, and infinite love resonates with you most deeply and opens your heart. This could be a religious or spiritual figure such as Buddha or Jesus, or perhaps a spiritual teacher.

If you do not have a specific religious affiliation or cannot relate to spiritual figures, don't worry. Simply visualize pure golden light in the sky before you. If you cannot picture this presence clearly in your mind, just feel the presence, and consider and trust that it is there.

Focus your mind and heart on the presence you have invoked.

Next, imagine that this infinitely loving, compassionate, and wise presence is deeply moved by your heartfelt and sincere wish. The presence looks at you with a loving, warm gaze and, from its heart, sends out love and compassion in the form of a stream of rays of golden light. These light rays touch all aspects of your being. Strongly feel that they reach the deepest corners of your mind and heart, the places touched by illness or where there is fear of illness.

As these light rays keep streaming down to you, visualize that they heal whatever it is that needs healing. Imagine that they offer forgiveness, understanding, and peace. Consider that they are healing any past negativity, troubling history, unfinished business, destructive emotions, and pain—including any deeper, hidden sources of your suffering.

It is good to really spend time with this portion of the practice—to truly open up and receive these blessings. This is especially important when you feel a lack of love, are torn up by despair and fear, are anxious that some things you might have done or said are unforgiveable, or when you struggle to forgive others.

At the end of the practice, imagine that your entire being is completely healed by the light streaming from this presence. Every single cell of your body has been transformed and dissolved into a small sphere of light. This sphere now soars up into the sky and merges inseparably with the heart of the presence that you have been visualizing.

Take time to rest in this state of oneness for as long as possible before you conclude the meditation.

You can do this practice for shorter or longer periods. In the beginning, it is good to spend some time becoming familiar with this meditation before you do it for someone else. A friend who had been caring for her ill husband at home for many years shared that she did this practice whenever she felt closed in or desperate, "For me, the practice is just knowing that the great spiritual beings are always here, ready to love and help us. It's like, they know our condition, they know our problems. They can see the pain and the human condition. They have that tremendous warmth and care and a real wish to benefit beings. I have come to know and trust that. I used to feel this very strongly doing the Essential Phowa practice; I would just get this tremendous feeling of being cared for, just this feeling of light pouring into me."

If you do the practice for another person, you don't have to be in their presence. The beautiful thing is that you can offer this meditation from a distance, wherever you are. If you are at the bedside of a dying person and the person is open and interested, you can share the Essential Phowa with them. Let them know that that the practice can be adapted in ways that are personally meaningful.

ESSENTIAL PHOWA FOR SOMEONE WHO IS ILL OR DYING

Essential Phowa can be very beneficial for someone who is ill or dying. You can also do the practice right after someone has died, over the following days or weeks, or long after.

When you are practicing for someone else, the steps to follow are basically the same as when you are practicing for yourself. The only difference is that you visualize the embodiment of truth, wisdom, and compassion above the head of the person.

From the depth of your heart, ask for guidance and support for this person who is sick, dying, or has died. Then imagine rays of light pouring from the presence down to that person. Consider that the light brings healing to any physical, emotional, or mental pain and suffering the person may have experienced throughout their life, and it brings healing to illness as well, including the hidden sources of suffering. Imagine these light rays healing any suffering they have experienced during their dying and the moment of death. Keep invoking the grace and blessing of the compassionate, loving presence for as long as you wish. Imagine the person's entire being is enveloped by the healing light, and gradually transformed by it.

At the end of the meditation, visualize the dying person dissolving into light and becoming one with the heart of the radiant presence.

At death, according to the Tibetan Buddhist teachings, the ordinary, thinking mind driven by anger, desire, and ignorance dies, and what is laid bare is the true essence of mind, beyond thoughts and emotions. If we recognize this essence, liberation, it is said, is possible. This essence is likened to the quality and experience of a cloudless sky—open, clear, and spacious. Christian contemplatives and many mystical traditions have different names for this deeper reality, "God," "the Divine," or "the Hidden Essence." In Buddhism, it is called buddha nature, the nature of our mind, the ground luminosity, or clear light.

Being in Mary's presence at the moment of her death and in the moments following her death, and feeling the profound peace, warmth, and clarity in the room, I wondered if she had caught a glimpse of this luminosity that contemplative practitioners over the ages have experienced.

9

The Gifts of Accompanying the Dying

The denial of death is a powerful force. Even after all these years of working in end-of-life care, when I reflect on my own death, I can still catch myself quietly thinking not about *when* I die, but *if* I die. The reality of my own death hit me one July afternoon nearly twenty-five years ago. Even though I had been at the bedside of many dying people by that time, I had still managed to shield myself from the painful fact that one day it would be me lying there on the bed. I was with Mai-Lee, a lady in her late fifties, her petite body completely emaciated by cancer. I tried to help her prop herself up in bed. With a shrug of her shoulders she glanced at her bony hand, and lifting up her head, her big, dark eyes looked straight at me. Her glance was naked, piercing, free of any inhibitions. At that moment, as I held her gaze, the painful truth of my own death hit me with full and direct force. I saw my future reflected in her eyes.

This existence of ours is as transient as autumn clouds.
To watch the birth and death of beings is like looking at
    the movements of a dance.
A lifetime is like a flash of lightning in the sky,
Rushing by, like a torrent down a steep mountain.

                        —Buddha Shakyamuni

Sitting with someone who is terminally ill is a profound contemplation on our own mortality and shared human frailty. It is as if we are looking into the fierce mirror of our own reality. The illness of the other, their vulnerability and death, is our own. In the beginning, it is deeply challenging and unsettling to confront this truth. But with time, it is possible to turn toward it, with less fear and even with confidence.

To be with the dying is to be with our *own* dying. It is an incredible opportunity, if we can see it this way—instead of continuously turning away from the fear of death, to mindfully turn toward it. The truth is we are all dying, we just don't know when or how. It is one thing to understand this truth intellectually, but another to actually feel it in your bones. In my work, I found that it is essential to shed light on one's fears and beliefs, however "irrational" they may be, as one's attitude colors one's perceptions and actions. For example, there is the irrational fear that talking about death openly will bring about one's death.

Our fears are what prevent us from feeling at ease within ourselves, and at ease around the dying. As long as we avoid the realities of death, suffering, and loss, and are reluctant to look at our own mortality, being in the presence of a loved one or patient who is ill or dying will always be terrifying.

This may sound surprising, but death and dying are in fact about life and living. In the presence of death, life unexpectedly becomes vibrant and rich. Within the pain and sadness of the impending loss of those we care for, the smile in their eyes or the sound of them sleeping peacefully transform into the most sacred and precious thing. Daring to be present for the dying, we have the opportunity to become present, open, and aware, and wake up to see, perhaps for the first time, the preciousness of this human life of ours.

> Death is our friend precisely because it brings us into absolute and passionate presence with all that is here, that is natural, that is love.
>
> —Rainer Maria Rilke, letter to Countess Margot Sizzo-Noris-Crouy, from *A Year with Rilke*

Death challenges us to be fully present in the nakedness of the present moment, to let go of the need for control in situations that we cannot control, and to realize and accept our own powerlessness. We can learn to see what is really true, what matters, and who we are beyond this body and this life. *If everything changes and dies, what can I truly rely on? What is my inner source of trust and strength, my place of refuge?*

Ironically, to accompany the dying and still care against the background of our own powerlessness has a powerful effect. Once we stop pouring our energy into avoidance and learn to accept death, this acceptance becomes a strength; and it is a strength that others can draw from. So, as much as possible, do not try to protect yourself from death. Befriend it in whatever small ways you can. Allow death to touch you and open your heart. We are all in this together. Death is a universal experience, and with every passing moment we move closer to it. When we acknowledge this truth, not only on an intellectual level but by learning to live with it in a deeply felt, personal, and experiential way, we touch the ground of compassion. Compassion is about fearlessness. It is about having the courage to go toward something that normally we would fear.

Accompanying a dying person, we offer our body, our speech, and our mind, and we offer our skills and knowledge. We offer our physical strength when the person needs a stable arm. We offer words of comfort, or we listen in silence with tenderness and love. We share our mind's clarity in the midst of emotional upheaval and mental confusion. But we are not the only ones who give in a caring relationship. In sharing their experience, the dying person gives as well; and in this process of *giving and receiving*, we are transformed as well.

There will always be a tremendous temptation to ignore our own relationship to death. It is so easy to slip into the role of *the helper*, with the seemingly selfless, yet dualistic attitude of "*I* am helping *you*." In this role, dying and death happen to the other person, and thankfully not us. We operate under the illusion that we are "bulletproof"—death, pain, and suffering cannot touch us. We either objectify or victimize the dying person, so as not to be touched by their suffering and pain. This person becomes someone in need of rescue or charity.

Sadly, instead of protecting us, this strategy cuts us off from our good heart and the possibility of making a genuine connection. The dying person, who is already extremely vulnerable, feels, as discussed earlier, not seen and even more disempowered, ashamed, and embarrassed; and we, the companion, end up feeling disconnected, resentful, and burnt out. Naturally, we all like to be comfortable, but unless we let go of this, there is the risk that accompanying those who are dying will be more about our need to feel comfortable than theirs.

The fear of death along with the fear of suffering, if we don't work with it in a compassionate and kind way for ourselves, will cause distress and, in the long run, burnout.

May the nourishment of the earth be yours,
May the clarity of light be yours,
May the fluency of the ocean be yours,
May the protection of the ancestors be yours.

And so may a slow
Wind work these words
Of love around you,
An invisible cloak
To mind your life.

> —from "A Blessing for the New Year"
> John O'Donohue, *To Bless the Space between Us*

For as long as space exists
And sentient beings endure,
May I too remain,
To dispel the misery of the world.

> —Shantideva, *The Way of the Bodhisattva*

Being in the presence of death can bring up the deepest questions and thus be a powerful catalyst to finally make peace—even friends—with death, and consequently with life. Acknowledging our fear of death is the first and, I believe, the most important step to moving toward a sense of acceptance and understanding. Spending some time reflecting, meditating, journaling, or in conversations with like-minded others who are exploring this challenging topic, in an open and unafraid way, I know from my own experience, can be incredibly supportive and liberating.

In the midst of the chaos, emotional turmoil, and often poignant and painful sense of groundlessness, a tender kindness toward ourselves, acceptance, and understanding help us to be fundamentally okay with whatever we experience and relax with who we are. We can come to discover our natural ground and true nature, one that is inherently stable and at the same time open, clear, spacious, and deeply compassionate; one that allows us to live fully and fearlessly—to "dance with change." This discovery is the greatest gift and final treasure that comes from daring to be present with and walking alongside the dying.

GRATITUDE

Writing, like dying, is by its nature a solitary experience. The process, however, doesn't have to be. Putting words onto paper or, more accurately, onto the screen, I had many companions walking alongside me throughout this exhilarating and also challenging journey. To my companions—my colleagues who carry their hearts in their hands; the faculty of Authentic Presence and its graduates who make a real difference in their communities in North America, Australia, Europe, rural India, or Argentina; the wonderful teams serving in the Spiritual Care Programme around the globe; my mentors; my spiritual, writer, and artist friends; my family and my loving husband—thanks for being there. Thank you to the enthusiastic and skilled team at Shambhala Publications. In profound gratitude to all my teachers: without your kindness, my mind would still be stubborn and narrow, and my heart comfortably small.

Without your inspiration, I would have never dared to enter this work, let alone write about it. May your wisdom continue to shine in this world.

Being with dying, I learned to hold space for irreconcilable states—sorrow and joy, quiet happiness and grief. I have deep gratitude to those I have accompanied over the years and who have allowed me to be present through their time of dying: for the joy, laughter, tears, deep connections, and your patience for the moments when I was not as skillful and wise as you expected me to be from years of sitting on my cushion. In your dying, you taught me about life and, most importantly, about the infinite and timeless power of love. May you be at peace, may you be free.

In memory of my beloved great-grandmother Marie, my grandma and grandpa, and my mother.

This book is dedicated to you.

SIGNS THAT DEATH DRAWS NEAR

Ann Allegre, MD, and Beate Dirkschnieder are educators in the Spiritual Care Programme. Ann is a palliative-care physician in Kansas; Beate works as a hospice social worker in Germany. Between them, they have many years of experience. I asked them to share their knowledge and insights about the common signs and symptoms of approaching death. Having a basic understanding of what to expect and the expert support from your health-care provider, palliative-care, and hospice team can help to lessen anxieties and avoid the risk of a last-minute panic.

How can we tell that death is near?

BEATE: "How long does my loved one have left to live?" This is a frequently asked question, and the answer is that none of us can know. A person may die much faster than expected, or live on for weeks or even months. It is difficult to know exactly when someone is dying. Each death is unique. Yet there are common physical and nonphysical signs that tell us death is near. These may occur months before the end of life or just in the final few days.

ANN: Most people with an advanced illness have increasing weakness over time, requiring more help and support from those around them. At first, they may just need help getting out of the house or taking a bath. Later, they may need twenty-four-hour assistance because they are no longer able to get up from a chair or walk without help. They require assistance with dressing, preparing food, and getting to the toilet. Eventually, most people are too weak to get out of bed and perhaps even to turn themselves in bed. They may have difficulty feeding themselves and even swallowing. Their voice may be too weak to be understood, and they might find it difficult to even keep their eyes open because of their weakness.

Along with physical weakness, those who are dying may have less and less energy for activities that they used to manage easily. How can we best support them at that stage?

ANN: It is important to conserve energy, giving priority to the activities that are most important to the person. Some hospice nurses tell patients, "Consider that you have a dollar's worth of energy per day. It might take twenty cents to take a shower and thirty cents to visit with a friend for a half hour. Make sure that you get the most out of what you have."

Most people spend longer periods of time sleeping, often with frequent naps, and they feel the need to rest after any significant activity. Eventually, they may spend most of their time sleeping. Near the end of life, when they are bedbound and lack the energy even to keep their eyes open most of the time, it can be difficult to tell if they are sleeping or lying there with their eyes closed. Always assume that they can hear and understand the conversations going on around them, even if they don't respond.

So often, we show our love by preparing and sharing meals together, but when nearing the end of life, a person may have less desire for food. This can be hard for people around the dying. What advice would you give them?

ANN: Most people with progressive illness have less and less desire for food. This is often a great concern for loved ones, who feel that the dying person is weaker because of a lack of intake. However, experience has shown that forcing someone to eat more or feeding that person artificially (such as intravenously) does not improve the weakness in most cases, and can lead to new complications such as swelling, nausea, and congestion. Surprisingly, some people have lived for weeks or months on mere sips of fluids and bites to eat.

The best approach for decreasing appetite is to provide foods that are appealing to patients in the amounts that they can eat. As a hospice nurse said, "If they only feel like eating two peas, just put two peas on the plate." Just seeing a large plate of food can take away their appetite. Many will find that fruity flavors and easily digestible foods are more appealing than heavy meals. When they request a favorite food, they may feel they have had enough after a few bites. Families should offer food and drinks frequently, without badgering patients to eat or getting into conflicts about whether they are eating enough.

Near the end of life, most people develop trouble with swallowing due to their extreme weakness and sleepiness. They can choke when swallowing. They should be given food and fluids only when they are awake, and should be upright when trying to swallow, if possible. Small sips and bites of soft foods may be easier to swallow. If they have coughing spells with intake, patients should be allowed to choose whether they want to continue to try to eat or drink. Thickeners may be added to fluids to make them easier to swallow, but many people prefer to continue with regular "thin" liquids. When people are not able to swallow at all, it is still important to keep their mouth moist and clean by using moistened mouth swabs. The swabs can be dipped into a drink that the patient enjoys, allowing them to enjoy the flavor.

What about changes in breathing? Many families and friends say that this is often the most difficult and distressing change to witness.

ANN: Shortness of breath is a common symptom at the end of life, especially prevalent in diseases affecting the heart and lungs but present in many other situations. The cause of the shortness of breath should be sought and addressed directly by a medical professional when possible, such as reducing congestion or draining fluid that has accumulated around the lungs. In many cases, there is no cause that can be addressed. Breathlessness can be treated with medications, and oxygen supplementation is appropriate if oxygen levels are low. For family members, the biggest support they can offer is reassuring the dying person through their presence, affection, and love. Other things family members can do to help the feeling of breathlessness are to use a fan to move the air, keep the room cool, allow space around the person or a view of outdoors, and position the person in the way that is most comfortable for their breathing and based on the instruction by medical caregivers.

Near the end of life, especially in the final hours or few days, many people have more irregular breathing patterns. This is often seen as periods of deep breathing which gradually slow and taper off, leading to a brief gap in breathing. These gaps, called apnea, often last for fifteen to twenty seconds, but they can go for over a minute. They do not seem to cause any discomfort to the patient but can be distressing to loved ones who fear that the patient won't breathe again. If patients are having these periods of apnea while they are responsive, they seem to become briefly unaware during the apnea but then return to their previous level of response.

Some people have congestion in their upper airway near the end of life, causing loud congestion with breathing. This is sometimes called the death rattle. The best way to help this is to turn the patient onto their side so that the congestion drains out from the back of their throat into the mouth. Medications may also help with the congestion, and the mouth should be kept clean with swabs. This congestion is difficult to listen to, but does not cause the dying person to feel significantly short of breath.

Are there any other signs that we need to be aware of during the final days?

ANN: Many people develop changes in skin color and temperature, especially in the final days of life. Earlier in the illness, people may appear pale or develop dark circles under their eyes as signs of ill-health. Near the end, the skin may be quite cool, particularly on the hands and feet. In many cases, dark purple splotchy areas, called mottling, appear in these cold areas. This appears to be related to decreased blood flow to the skin. It often occurs at a time when blood pressure is quite low and the pulse is weak. Even though these changes sometimes indicate that death is near, they are occasionally reversible—areas that were cold and mottled may become warm and pink.

BEATE: Beyond these physical changes, it is crucial to look at the person's behavior and mental frame of mind: How does the person view their life? Is there anything that needs to be done? Is there a sense of acceptance? Does the person openly speak of their coming death? Are there unresolved things? Is there anything holding the person back? People can mobilize enormous forces within themselves to prolong their dying. One of my hospice patients was a single mother. Her son was grown up and she was expecting her first grandchild. No one believed that she would live to see the baby's birth, but she was adamant that she would. She actually lived for another six months and died two days after her granddaughter was born.

The time of death is also influenced by the degree to which loved ones accept the reality of the impending death. If family members can allow for the natural dying process to happen and tell the dying person that it is okay for them to let go, while assuring the person of their love, it will be easier for the dying person to make peace with death.

A dying person can go through profound mental and emotional changes, including spiritual distress. What is your experience?

ANN: Many people experience significant emotional symptoms due to severe illness, including anxiety and depression. Most dying people experience appropriate grief due to their circumstances, but some develop clinical depression. The medical professionals working with the patient can help to determine whether treatment for depression is needed.

BEATE: Some people will experience various types of spiritual distress such as questioning their faith, feeling there is no meaning in life, wondering why they have to suffer, or the existential distress of wondering what becomes of them after death. Their distress should be addressed directly through offering supportive listening or engaging the support of the pastoral-care provider or representative of their faith tradition. They may also need medications to control emotional symptoms and provide more immediate relief.

ANN: It is also common for dying people to develop withdrawal, confusion, and memory loss. They are usually no longer interested in topics that are more peripheral to their situation, such as current events, and are more focused on immediate concerns. In some cases, they may develop symptoms that are more disturbing, such as frightening hallucinations, severe agitation, paranoia, and combativeness. This delirium can make it challenging to manage care, and requires good medical support to control symptoms. Delirium can occur owing to the type of disease (such as brain tumors or dementia) but can also be brought on by medications, uncontrolled pain, and other factors. Whenever possible, the causative factor should be addressed. People with delirium should be treated in a quiet and soothing environment; many will also need medications for the symptoms.

A dying person may see a loved one who has died or a spiritual figure at the bedside. These experiences can be easily dismissed as hallucinations.

BEATE: At the border between life and death, the perception of reality often changes. Sometimes levels of our habitual reality intermingle with that of another reality. These visions are often comforting to people who are dying. They most commonly occur near the end of life, but can occur weeks or months ahead of death. These experiences can help them to reconcile and come to peace with their life and to prepare for their death.

When ordinary language fails, the dying may communicate through gestures or metaphors, such as going on a boat trip or train ride. One dying father told his daughter shortly before he died, "You can get the car, we can drive now." Another dying man in our hospice said, "I do not know whether I belong here, or in another room." He died three days later.

Other examples that I have heard from hospice patients are: "I'm standing in a long line and still have to wait," "I have to cross a river," or a classic one, "I want to go home." Home in this case doesn't necessarily refer to their physical home, but their home in a deeper spiritual sense. We need to listen for these kinds of hidden messages and try to decipher them in order to avoid isolation and misunderstanding. Yet all too often, things may only become clear in retrospect, after the person has died. I find it helpful to step into the image the person uses, and notice what it evokes in me. This can reveal a source of distress, or an unexpressed fear or need that the person has.

Some of the changes during the dying process seem to happen slowly over a long period of time, while others seem to come on suddenly. Death, even when it is expected and hospice involved, still seems to come as a surprise. A dying person can rally and appear like they are actually getting better. How can we deal with some of the confusion and the many uncertainties and changes?

ANN: All of the symptoms we have described can come and go during the ups and downs over the course of decline. Sometimes the dying person seems to be very close to death but then rallies and shows improvement. This up-and-down course can be stressful for all involved, and create confusion about how much longer the person can live. Sometimes this leads to inappropriate hope of recovery; sometimes it can lead to frustration that the dying process will continue for longer than expected. It can be helpful to recall that the overall trend is downward and to recognize that a relatively good day is an opportunity for connection and meaning, a gift that may not come again.

Here is a list of some of the signs and symptoms that death is imminent:

- Increased weakness and dependence on others; the dying person is less and less able to get out of bed or out of a chair, spends more time in bed, gets sleepier, and refuses to eat and drink.
- The dying person may have a sudden wish to reconcile with estranged family members or to put personal and family affairs in order.
- A dying person who has been previously confused, semiconscious, or unconscious may unexpectedly become lucid for a few days or hours. They may rally enough to communicate and say goodbye.
- Those who are dying may muster incredible hidden strengths to wait for the arrival of a relative before they die. They may also wait for relatives and friends to leave, so they can die in peace without anyone holding them back.
- Those who are dying may experience profound waking or sleeping dreams. They may see loved ones

who have died, or spiritual figures at the bedside. Don't dismiss these experiences as hallucinations. These experiences can help them to reconcile and come to peace with their life and to prepare for their death.

CONSIDERATIONS FOR
ADVANCE HEALTH-CARE DIRECTIVES

An advance health-care directive (also known as an advance directive or living will) allows those who are dying to inform family members and health-care professionals ahead of time of their wishes for the end of life, in case they cannot any longer communicate their wishes. As mentioned earlier in the book, providing detailed instructions on creating advance health-care directives is beyond the scope of this book and should be discussed with a legal professional. Given my long work in end-of-life care and the work of many colleagues in the Spiritual Care Programme, I offer some considerations that aren't always included in advance health-care directives but can make the dying process easier for everyone.

Since most health-care directives do not include details of what people would like in their hospital room, or their spiritual-care needs, you may consider encouraging them to add their responses to these questions to whichever health-care-directive form they decide to use. Be sure to write down the name and contact information of a spiritual friend, clergy, or religious organization that could provide whatever support they request. Once completed, the health-care directive should be reviewed and updated regularly to ensure that the information remains correct. In addition to recording the wishes of the person who is dying, make sure to discuss them with rest of the family and anyone who is likely to be involved in the person's care.

SPIRITUAL-CARE WISHES

You might consider adding information about spiritual care wishes to the advance health-care directive. Topics might include:

- Do you have a regular spiritual practice, a "heart practice"?
- Are there images or photographs that you would like within eyesight (or on the ceiling if you must lie flat)?
- Is there anything else you would like, or not like, in your room?
- When you are near to death, are there special practices that you would like to have done at your side, or elsewhere?

- What music, chants, prayers, or teachings—if any— would you most like to hear?
- Is there one special person, or a few people, whom you want to be near you for support? (Be sure to write their names and telephone numbers in the health-care directive.)
- Are there any spiritual practices or charitable actions that you would like to have sponsored in your name, either before or after your death?

IF FILLING OUT A FORM IS DIFFICULT

Many people find filling out a form difficult for a variety of reasons. There are a number of creative ways for family members, friends, or care providers to overcome the initial hesitation or resistance that can come up.

- Take time to fill out the form together with them, over the course of a day or a couple of afternoons. In my experience, this has proved to be the most successful technique.
- Encourage them to fill in sections they feel clear about for now.
- Interview them and record their answers.

When a dying person expresses their wishes for end-of-life care, this can sometimes be difficult for us to hear. If you are having a hard time with some of the wishes, you might try one of the practices from chapter 3 to help you return to your body and your breath, to notice what you're feeling, or to find peace.

In addition to a formal document that outlines the wishes of those who are dying, informal documents that record their loves, passions, and relationships can be invaluable. If they are still able to write or speak, you can also suggest that they write personal letters to loved ones, especially children, in the file with their documented wishes, forms, and other papers. They could also include letters that they have saved and treasured over the years. A letter expressing their personal thoughts, love, and appreciation could turn out to be a legacy that is treasured above all others.

RESOURCES

END OF LIFE

Caring Connections

Sponsored by the National Hospice and Palliative Care organization. It offers information on advance-care planning, caregiving, bereavement, and hospice services.

www.caringinfo.org

The Conversation Project

The Conversation Project is a public engagement initiative with a goal to have every person's wishes for end-of-life care expressed and respected.

https://theconversationproject.org/about/

European Association for Palliative Care

Website includes directories of hospice and palliative-care programs from many countries, as well as some documents in multiple languages.

www.eapcnet.eu

Hospice Foundation of America

Provides resources to locate hospice care and information on caregiver support.

www.hospicefoundation.org

Hospice Net

Provides information about hospice for patients and care-givers.

www.hospice.net

International Association for Hospice and Palliative Care

A global nonprofit dedicated to promoting palliative care around the world. The website has a tool to translate into multiple languages. The association publishes a free monthly newsletter online that addresses the challenges with getting access to palliative care in various countries.

www.hospicecare.com

MedlinePlus

Medline is the National Institutes of Health's website for patients and their families and friends.

medlineplus.gov

The National Hospice and Palliative Care Organization (NHPCO)

www.nhpco.org

The National Institute on Aging

www.nia.nih.gov/health/end-of-life

Palliative-Care Doctors

The patient site of the American Academy of Hospice and Palliative Medicine (AAHPM)

palliativedoctors.org

PRACTICAL CAREGIVER SUPPORT

Caring Bridge

Helps you to stay connected with loved ones during times of serious illness or crisis. You create a personalized website that shares news and allows people to post messages of support.

www.caringbridge.org

Lotsa Helping Hands

Helps you to organize a community with a versatile calendar function so people can sign up to offer help.

www.lotsahelpinghands.com

BEREAVEMENT

GriefNet

Online support, including discussion groups and other resources for people dealing with grief and loss.

www.griefnet.org

Compassionate Friends

Offers bereavement support to families who have experienced the death of a child.

www.compassionatefriends.org

Rainbows

Helps children deal with grief due to death, divorce, or separation. Offers programs nationwide.

www.rainbows.org

FILMS

Departures

A Japanese film about a young man who becomes a *nokanshi*, a traditional Japanese ritual mortician. Based on the biographical book *Coffinman*.

Cherry Blossoms

A German film about a terminally ill man taking a trip to Japan following the death of his wife.

Wit

The story of a female professor dying of breast cancer in a hospital. Based on a Pulitzer Prize–winning play.

CREDITS

BIBLIOGRAPHY

Bass, Ellen. *The Human Line*. Port Townsend, WA: Copper Canyon Press, 2007.

Bly, Robert. *Morning Poems*. New York: Harper, 1998.

Byock, Ira. *The Best Care Possible: A Physician's Quest to Transform Care through the End of Life*. New York: Avery, 2012.

———. *The Four Things That Matter Most: A Book about Living*. New York: Atria, 2014.

Callanan, Maggie, and Patricia Kelly. *Final Gifts: Understanding the Special Awareness, Needs, and Communications of the Dying*. New York: Simon and Schuster, 2012.

Chagdud Tulku Rinpoche. *Life in Relation to Death*. Junction City, CA: Padma Publishing, 2000.

Chödrön, Pema. *When Things Fall Apart: Heart Advice for Difficult Times.* Boston: Shambhala Publications, 1996.

Chökyi Nyima Rinpoche and David R. Shlim. *Medicine and Compassion: A Tibetan Lama's Guidance for Caregivers.* Boston: Wisdom Publications, 2006.

Dalai Lama. *Lojong: Training the Mind.* Boston: Wisdom Publications, 1999.

De Hennezel, Marie. *Intimate Death: How the Dying Teach Us How to Live.* New York: Vintage, 1998.

Dilgo Khyentse Rinpoche. *The Heart of Compassion.* Boston: Shambhala Publications, 2007.

Dzigar Kongtrul Rinpoche. *Training in Tenderness: Buddhist Teachings on Tsewa, the Radical Openness of Heart That Can Change the World.* Boulder: Shambhala Publications, 2018.

Ellison, Koshin Paley, and Matt Weingast. *Awake at the Bedside: Contemplative Teachings on Palliative and End-of-Life Care.* Somerville, MA: Wisdom Publications, 2016.

Fraser, Andy. *The Healing Power of Meditation: Leading Experts on Buddhism, Psychology, and Medicine Explore the Health Benefits of Contemplative Practice.* Boston: Shambhala Publications, 2013.

Gawande, Atul. *Being Mortal: Illness, Medicine, and What Matters at the End.* New York: Metropolitan Books, 2014.

Germer, Christopher. *The Mindful Path to Self-Compassion: Freeing Yourself from Destructive Thoughts and Emotions.* New York: The Guildford Press, 2009.

Gibran, Kahlil. *The Treasured Writings of Kahlil Gibran.* Reprint. Edison, NJ: Castle Books, 2009.

Giles, Cheryl A., and Willa B. Miller. *The Arts of Contemplative Care: Pioneering Voices in Buddhist Chaplaincy and Pastoral Work.* Somerville, MA: Wisdom Publications, 2012.

Halifax, Joan. *Being with Dying: Cultivating Compassion and Fearlessness in the Presence of Death.* Boston: Shambhala Publications, 2009.

Hanson, Rick, and Forrest Hanson. *Resilient: How to Grow an Unshakable Core of Calm, Strength, and Happiness.* New York: Harmony Books, 2018.

Kübler-Ross, Elisabeth. *On Death and Dying: What the Dying Have to Teach Doctors, Nurses, Clergy, and Their Own Families.* New York: Scribner, 2014.

Lief, Judith. *Making Friends with Death: A Buddhist Guide to Encountering Mortality.* Boston: Shambhala Publications, 2001.

Longaker, Christine. *Facing Death and Finding Hope: A Guide to the Emotional and Spiritual Care of the Dying.* New York: Doubleday, 1997.

Lynn, Joanne, Joan Harold, and Janice Lynn Schuster. *Handbook for Mortals: Guidance for People with Serious Illness.* Oxford: Oxford University Press, 2011.

Merton, Thomas. *Love and Living.* San Diego: Houghton Mifflin, 2007.

Merwin, W. S. *The Second Four Books of Poems.* Port Townsend, WA: Copper Canyon Press, 1993.

Neff, Kristin. *Self-Compassion: The Proven Power of Being Kind to Yourself.* New York: William Morrow, 2011.

Nelson, Portia. *There's a Hole in My Sidewalk: The Romance of Self-Discovery.* Hillsboro, OR: Beyond Words Publishing, 2018.

Nouwen, Henri. *Our Greatest Gift: A Meditation on Caring and Dying.* New York: Harper One, 2009.

———. *Reaching Out: Three Movements of the Spiritual Life.* New York: Doubleday, 1986.

Nye, Naomi Shihab. *Words under the Words: Selected Poems.* Portland, OR: The Eighth Mountain Press, 2001.

O'Donohue, John. *To Bless the Space between Us.* New York: Doubleday, 2008.

Oliver, Mary. *Dream Work.* New York: Grove/Atlantic, Inc., 1986.

Ostaseski, Frank. *The Five Invitations: Discovering What Death Can Teach Us about Living Fully.* New York: Flatiron Books, 2017.

Puchalski, Christina M., and Betty Ferrell. *Making Health Care Whole: Integrating Spirituality into Patient Care.* West Conshohocken, PA: Templeton Press, 2010.

———. *A Time for Listening and Caring: Spirituality and the Care of the Chronically Ill and Dying.* New York: Oxford University Press, 2006.

Ricard, Matthieu. *Altruism: The Power to Change Yourself and the World.* New York: Little, Brown and Company, 2015.

Rilke, Rainer Maria. *Letters to a Young Poet.* Translated by M. D. Herter Norton. New York: W. W. Norton & Company, 2004.

———. *A Year with Rilke: Daily Readings from the Best of Rainer Maria Rilke.* Translated and edited by Joanna Macy and Anita Barrows. New York: HarperOne, 2009.

Rumi. *The Essential Rumi.* Translated by Coleman Barks. New York: HarperCollins, 1995.

Salzberg, Sharon. *Loving-Kindness: The Revolutionary Art of Happiness.* Boston: Shambhala Publications, 2002.

Saunders, Cicely. *Watch with Me: Inspiration for a Life in Hospice Care.* Sheffield, UK: Mortal Press, 2003.

Shantideva. *The Way of the Bodhisattva: A Translation of the Bodhicharyavatara.* Padmakara Translation Group. Boston: Shambhala Publications, 1997.

Shabkar Tsogdruk Rangdrol. *The Life of Shabkar: Autobiography of a Tibetan Yogin*. Translated by Matthieu Ricard. Ithaca, NY: Snow Lion Publications, 2001.

Sheik, Anees A. *Healing Images: The Role of Imagination in Health*. Amityville, NY: Baywood Publishing, 2003.

Sogyal Rinpoche. *The Tibetan Book of Living and Dying*. 2nd ed. San Francisco: HarperCollins, 2002.

Thich Nath Hanh. *No Fear, No Death: Comforting Wisdom for Life*. New York: Riverhead Books, 2002.

Thondup, Tulku. *Peaceful Death, Joyful Rebirth: A Tibetan Buddhist Guidebook*. Boston: Shambhala Publications, 2006.

Trungpa, Chögyam. *Shambhala: The Sacred Path of the Warrior*. Boston: Shambhala Publications, 2015.

Tsoknyi Rinpoche and Eric Swanson. *Open Mind, Open Heart: Awakening the Power of Essence Love*. New York: Harmony Books, 2012.

Wyatt, Karen. *What Really Matters: 7 Lessons for Living from the Stories of the Dying*. 2nd edition. Silverhorn, CO: Sunroom Studios, 2015.

Yeats, W. B. *The Celtic Twilight: Faerie and Folklore*. Mineola, NY: Dover Publications, 2004.

———. *Collected Poems of W. B. Yeats*. London: Collector's Library, 2010.

Yongey Mingyur Rinpoche and Eric Swanson. *Joy of Living: Unlocking the Secret and Science of Happiness.* New York: Harmony Books, 2007.

Zimmerman, Jack, and Virginia Coyle. *The Way of Council.* 2nd ed. Colchester, UK: Bramble Books, 2009.

ABOUT THE AUTHOR

Kirsten DeLeo has accompanied terminally ill patients and their families for over twenty-five years. She is a teacher in the field of contemplative care and leads courses, workshops, and retreats worldwide. Kirsten helped to pioneer Authentic Presence, one of the first contemplative-based programs in end-of-life care in the United States, now offered in Ireland as well (authentic-presence.org). Kirsten is an international trainer with the Spiritual Care Programme (spcare.org), a network offering contemplative-based, nondenominational education in eleven countries. Kirsten is trained in the Hakomi mindfulness-based somatic approach to psychotherapy and has been immersed in Buddhist study and practice for over twenty years, including a three-year meditation retreat.